A

GOD

we can

TRUST

*A Pastor Offers Reassurance and Hope
In a Changed World*

LOREN
SEIBOLD

D0921054

Pacific Press® Publishing Association
Nampa, Idaho
Oshawa, Ontario, Canada
www.pacificpress.com

Edited by Bonnie Tyson-Flyn
Cover Design by Tim Larson
Cover photo by EyeWire ©
Inside Design by Steve Lanto

Copyright © 2002 by
Pacific Press® Publishing Association
Printed in the United States of America
All Rights Reserved

Additional copies of this book may be purchased at
http://www.adventistbookcenter.com

ISBN 0-8163-1928-6

02 03 04 05 06 • 5 4 3 2 1

CONTENTS

INTRODUCTION

It was the loveliest of early-autumn mornings. A large old walnut tree hovers over our back-yard deck. My favorite deck chair, a cup of tea, and a good book beneath the tree always begin my warm-season days. This is how I collect scattered threads of thought, say my prayers, count my blessings, and anticipate the day. Between pages I wander the garden, fingers wrapped around a warm cup, as I check for new shoots, fruit, or blossoms.

Each season has its joy. In spring, as soon as the weather warms, I emerge wrapped in fleece and cap, to look for crocuses and daffodils. My reading is often short, and my steaming drink cools quickly. Summer offers cloying yet comforting heat and dozens of rose blossoms.

Autumn is best. There is a sensation one gets—the sun at a low angle, a golden light, falling leaves, the chill that delightfully disturbs your complacency with the promise of winter. There is an edginess to winter that comes with the sense that one's comfortable outdoor world is soon to undergo a rather dramatic change.

Thus my thoughts and feelings on the morning of September 11, 2001. I finished my meditations, gathered my daily office-bound cargo—a Palm Pilot®, sunglasses, keys, assorted books and papers that have made their way home but don't belong there—and got into my Chevy pickup. National Public Radio came on with the turn of the key. My first stirring of concern came not from hearing any specific news, but from unfamiliarity; the voices I hear each morning weren't there. The speakers sounded upset, stressed. A reporter was talking to a person on a telephone—a midstream conversation whose meaning I couldn't decipher. "In case you're just tuning in," someone said at last, "two hijacked jetliners have been flown into the World Trade Center. Thousands are feared dead."

A shiver ran up my back, into my shoulders. I wasn't sure I believed what I'd just heard. This isn't the sort of thing that happens here! It happens in the plot of a Tom Clancy novel, perhaps, but not in real life! For a moment I entertained the possibility that I was listening to a radio drama, perhaps a modern analog to the 1938 radiobroadcast of a dramatization of H. G. Wells's *The War of the Worlds* that caused mass hysteria throughout North America.

But it was not fiction. It was real life. Painfully, desperately real. Real people with families, jobs, churches, children. Real people, atomized by the force of Boeings striking concrete at hundreds of miles per hour. Real people crushed by tons of stones. Real people burned and suffocated.

Over 3,000 real people. Dead. Within an hour.

In the weeks since, we have learned more. Yet the shock has never gone away. I know where I was when President Kennedy was shot (in my fourth-grade music class), when Neil Armstrong stepped on the moon (by the table in my parents' kitchen), and when my mother said my father was dying of cancer (on a portable phone in my yard).

Now I can add one more to the list: I was riding in a Chevrolet pickup, on my way to my church office, when I learned that America had been hit by the biggest terrorist attack in modern history.

THE QUESTIONS

I am a minister of a church. As a minister, I have the privilege of sharing with people in significant passages of their lives—both the joyous and the difficult. I also discuss with them some of the hard questions. I can confidently say my parishioners have taught me more than I have taught them, both by thoughtful words and cautionary examples.

On the evening of September 11, 2001, I gathered with my church family in the sanctuary of our small colonial-style church. Together we prayed, grieved, expressed our fears, and comforted one another. People came in with tears and left with them. I found that for most of my church members, their response to the tragedies of September 11, 2001, was a flood of questions. Where was God? How could He let this happen? Will we ever have peace and safety again? What kind of people would do such a thing? And should we really love them, as Jesus said? Is this a sign of the end? What if we have to go to war?

As their pastor, I found myself searching for answers to their questions. I have found the answer to be simple, yet (paradoxically) sometimes extraordinarily difficult to put into practice. The answer is this: We must trust God. Even when tragedies darken our skies. Even when we glimpse the darkness in the hearts of our fellow human beings. Even when the future is clouded with fear. Even when God's purposes are unknown to us, His interactions with His world obscured from human eyes. For we serve a God we can trust. A God we can trust completely, implicitly, and absolutely. A God who "will never leave you nor forsake you" (Deuteronomy 31:6, NIV)—ever. The question we need not raise is whether God is trustworthy. That He is, is a certainty.

What we speak of rather, in books like this one, is the difficult process of actually learning to trust Him. How we, limited and broken and short-sighted human beings, can find comfort in God's strength even when He seems distant from us, when He seems silent or too transcendent to be interested in what is happening here.

This book takes as its starting point the events of September 11, 2001. These terrorist acts were not the first great tragedy of human existence, nor will they be the last. Wars and terrorism have long scarred the human race; they will again. And though wars and terrorism will likely affect but few of us, there is not a life but is at some point touched by pain.

What I have found (and I think you will, as well) is that life's tragedies differ little, except in scale, from one another. The answers to life's massive tragedies and to life's personal tragedies are really the same. The death of a young father in a crashing jetliner and the death of love between a husband and wife have the same explanation: evil is at work in the world. And death on a battlefield and a death from a heart attack can be met with the same remedy: We must trust our trustworthy God.

We shall find peace as we learn to believe that God loves us, even when tragedy overtakes us, and that He will at the end of all things make it right to us. He is—let there be no doubt in your heart—a God we can trust.

Where Was God?

At first consideration, it may sound an insolent question. Who are we, after all, to question God? It is a question that one imagines coming from the mouth of a cynic—shouting, in mockery, "Ha! Where's your God now?"

Skeptics have asked it often. But so have believers. It is a question, I have learned, that can emerge from the hearts of folks who have spent their lives trusting Heaven's care and beneficence.

And I would not be at all surprised if the same question was not in your mind on September 11, 2001. Where was God when buildings came tumbling down?

A Permitted Question

The Scripture rightly warns against arrogantly questioning God. "Be not rash with your mouth, nor let your heart be hasty to utter a word before God," warns the preacher of Ecclesiastes, "for God is in heaven, and you upon earth" (Ecclesiastes 5:2, RSV). The book of Job (though occasionally obscured by its poetic complexity) contains a similar challenge: How can human beings even begin to understand God, much less question His interaction in human affairs? Job seems, at times, scolded by God for simply wanting to know why he'd been singled out as the subject of an experiment between competing spiritual powers.

So if not insolent, it is at least a risky question—and I would shy from it completely were it not for someone else who asked this question. Someone with greater authority than any who wrote in the Hebrew testament of Scripture. Someone whose blend of humanity and divinity gives Him marvelous sympathy with human beings.

For this is a question asked by Jesus Himself. As He hung on the cross, His breath squeezed from His lungs by suspension of His entire body from His hands, He mustered a final painful breath to quote a line from a psalm (Psalm 22:1) that asked the one question that He *had* to speak aloud. The single question that tortured His soul even more than the nails tortured His body: *"E'loi, E'loi, lama sabachtha'ni?"* He cried. "My God, my God, why have you forsaken me?" (Matthew 27:46, NIV; Mark 15:34, NIV).

I struggle to understand how Jesus could have had any doubts of God's presence. For several years He had seen the most visible manifestations of God that anyone who has ever lived in a mortal body had been privileged to see: daily miracles, the audible voice of God, angels in heavenly brilliance before Him, translated saints in conversation with Him. And the accounts of the four evangelists are merely representative of a much more extensive heavenly rapport, for John asserts that "there are also many other things" that transpired in the life of Jesus (John 21:25, RSV), too many to be recorded. Such glorious faith-building events must have been His daily experience.

And yet faced with questions too big to understand, experiencing the pain of execution and the worse pain of the death of His hopes and dreams for the people He loved, even Jesus doubted the presence of His Father. *Why doesn't God stop this from happening? Why doesn't He spare Me this pain?*

If Jesus can ask such questions, then so can you and I. His question gives permission for ours. He reminds us that viewed through

WHERE WAS GOD? • 11

human eyes (human eyes like Jesus Himself looked through when God became human), the workings of the spiritual world are much harder to discern. That is why the God we serve does not prohibit us from questioning Him! For He knows that we humans are at a disadvantage when it comes to understanding the larger meaning of life's events. Unlike God, we don't know the end from the beginning. Unlike Jesus, we don't see the daily working of miraculous power. We are, on this nasty old earth, placed in the position of being asked to simply trust that all things will, in the end, work together for good to those who love Him.

One of the results of living in a world of sin is that the acts of Satan are often more evident in everyday life than the acts of God. Evil strikes us across the face; it maims our bodies, wounds our spirits, destroys relationships, and would, if it could, rip our confidence out by the roots. The enemy uses means unsubtle, audacious in their execution—methods that a good God cannot use.

And I have always believed that God understands that in the face of the horrifying onslaught of evil, faith is not easy for human beings. So let me assure you that it is neither trivial nor illegitimate to question God.

GOD WAS THERE

In the 1960s, the pronouncement that "God is dead" by a group of radical theologians became headline news. The phrase wasn't original with them; a bitter and disenchanted philosopher named Friedrich Nietzsche had pronounced God dead a century earlier.[1] Neither Nietzsche nor the later theologians thought that God had literally died; in fact, they believed that God had always been nothing but a myth and that in a scientific world, belief in God would inevitably die. They were wrong on the second count, of course: People have not ceased to believe in God.

But is God still with us? Even as airplanes crash into our nation's tallest buildings? As thousands of innocent, hard-working people are murdered? If not dead, did He abandon us, wicked and often failing human beings that we are, when we dropped atomic weapons on Nagasaki and Hiroshima, and murdered 6,000,000 Jews in World War II? Has He tired of our immorality, our materialism, our tendency to fight?

Perhaps this is hard to accept right now. But please believe me: God has been with us the entire time. He was there as the hijackers made their plans. As they took over the airplanes and flew them into buildings, killing thousands. As evil cowards dropped biologically contaminated letters into the mail. At each rescue. At each funeral. Each moment of each day, God was there.

How do I know?

Please don't think me dismissive of the difficulty of the question when I respond simply, "Because God has told me so."

"I am with you always, to the very end of the age" (Matthew 28:20, NIV), assured Jesus. Nothing "in all creation, will be able to separate us from the love of God" (Romans 8:39, NIV), insisted Paul. "Though the earth be removed, and though the mountains be carried into the midst of the sea" (Psalm 46:2, NKJV), promised the psalmist, God is there.

There is no more insightful testimony of God's omnipresence than the opening stanzas of Psalm 139. It begins with the psalmist's testimony that God knows each human being intimately.

O Lord, you have searched me and you know me.
You know when I sit and when I rise;
    you perceive my thoughts from afar.
You discern my going out and my lying down;
    you are familiar with all my ways (verses 1-3, NIV).

God is with people. He is with those who grieve. He is with those who are fearful, whose once-comfortable lives have been left in a state of agitation. He knows the hearts of those who suffer.

The day after the tragedy, one of my friends wondered aloud, "What must be in a person's heart to do something like this?" The thoughts of a person whose hatred exceeds any sense of the value of life eludes us. Yet it is not beyond the understanding of God. Though God is good, He does understand evil. That's why He hates it so much. God understood the hearts of the September 11 terrorists. He followed their plotting. He was aware of their plans. "Before a word is on my tongue you know it completely" (verse 4), said the psalmist. Sophisticated electronic scanners, telephone and email interceptions, and alert intelligence officers failed to hear those words. But God heard them.

The terrorists traveled all over the world—and with impunity in the United States. They managed to elude searchers and security officers at airports. They successfully hid from the most sophisticated scanners and the most experienced, shrewd intelligence operatives.

But they did not hide from God!

Where can I go from your Spirit?
Where can I flee from your presence?
If I go up to the heavens, you are there;
if I make my bed in the depths, you are there (verses 7, 8, NIV).

There is no place you can go where God is not present! And if God is present, then, in spite of the appearance of chaos, God's power is still at work as well.

Osama bin Laden may successfully hide in the mountains of Afghanistan. God has known all along where he was hiding. God knows his heart. And if there is left in him any trace of morality, any fiber of decency, any sense of the goodness of God (by whatever name he calls God), then I have no doubt that God is working on his heart.

> If I say, "Surely the darkness will hide me
>> and the light become night around me,"
> even the darkness will not be dark to you;
>> the night will shine like the day,
>> for darkness is as light to you (verses 11, 12, NIV).

Terrorists live in the darkness of secret hatreds, the darkness of camouflaged anger. The Islamic terrorists' instructions were to blend into the community, to be as inconspicuous as possible, while plotting the most horrible crimes conceivable.

They did not fool God. He followed them from the beginning of their hatreds. More, He followed them from the beginning of their lives!

> For you created my inmost being;
>> you knit me together in my mother's womb. . . .
> My frame was not hidden from you
>> when I was made in the secret place.
> When I was woven together in the depths of the earth,
>> your eyes saw my unformed body.
> All the days ordained for me were written in your book
>> before one of them came to be (verses 13-16, NIV).

God knew how the terrorists' lives would end. I have no doubt that until the very end, God was trying to change their minds.

If I can convince you of nothing else, I want you to know that tragedies, such as that which happened on September 11, 2001, do not indicate that God has abandoned this earth.

Faith, Not Feeling

We place a great deal of dependence on our feelings. To feel safe, to feel loved, to feel confident and assured—these are among life's great pleasures. Feeling fear, unhappiness, grief, and pain are among life's least pleasant experiences.

Our feelings affect us so strongly. Yet I have learned over time that it is not always safe to trust your feelings, for feelings are not always reliable. They can tell you that you are safe (as they did for the victims of the September 11 tragedy) when you are not. Conversely, they can tell you to fear when you are, in fact, in little danger—which has been the experience of millions who have been convinced, since September 11, 2001, against rational odds, that they are in danger of terrorists or anthrax.

Feelings are at times a useful barometer, but they're not infallible. Sometimes, in the midst of tragedy, our feelings can tell us that God is absent.

Well-known Christian teacher and writer C.S. Lewis had this experience. A devoted Christian, Lewis suddenly felt bereft of God's presence after losing his wife to cancer.

"Meanwhile, where is God?" he asked. "This is one of the most disquieting symptoms. When you are happy, so happy that you have no sense of needing Him, so happy that you are tempted to feel His claims upon you as an interruption, if you remember yourself and turn to Him with gratitude and praise, you will be—or so it feels—welcomed with open arms. But go to Him when your need is desperate, when all other help is vain, and what do you find? A door slammed in your face, and a sound of bolting. . . . After that, silence."

If you cannot trust your feelings, then what can you trust?

You can trust the promises of God. Our emotional perceptions can deceive us. But the fact of God's love and presence remains. He is here. And He is not silent.

God Is Not Silent

"It is fine to say God was there," complained one of my friends the day after the tragedy, "but why didn't He do something about it?"

How do you know He didn't?

It is fairly easy to show that the tragedies in New York and Washington, D.C., could have been much, much worse. Simple arithmetic will suffice.[2]

- The twin towers of the World Trade Center were places of employment for 50,000 people. Approximately 3,000 died in the buildings. So almost 95 percent of those targeted survived!
- The Pentagon employs about 23,000 people; yet only 123 lost their lives. That is a 99.5 percent survival rate.
- What about the airplanes? American Airlines Flight 77, the Boeing 757 that was crashed into the Pentagon, could have carried 289 people, yet only 64 were aboard. Seventy-eight percent of the seats were empty.
- Each of the two Boeing 767s that were piloted into the World Trade Center could have held 351 people. American Airlines Flight 11, carried 92—74 percent of the seats were empty. United Airlines Flight 175 contained 65 people—81 percent empty.
- United Airlines Flight 93 was a Boeing 757 that had only 45 people aboard—84 percent empty. In addition, these 45 resisted the hijackers, thereby laying down their lives to prevent the hijackers from hitting another target building.

Out of 74,280 people who might have been killed by these attacks, 95 percent survived!

Clearly, God was at work! And if He saved so many here, can you imagine how many other times He prevents tragedies? How many car accidents never happen? How many planes He holds up with a touch of His hand? How many nuclear power plant disasters were stopped by His finger preventing the leak? How many wars were averted that we didn't even know were brewing?

I've come to believe that if God weren't ceaselessly at work in our world, the human situation would be unendurable. Evil is an overwhelming force that wants nothing more than the utter destruction of all humanity. If it weren't for God's miraculous intervention, even now atomic weapons or biological warfare might have already destroyed this world. The hatred that breeds in the hearts of human beings might have broken so many of our relationships that hatred would rule all nations.

There is a picture in the book of Revelation of four angels holding back four winds (see Revelation 7:1, 3). The winds are a metaphor for the effects of evil: wars, terrorism, and tragedies. "Do not yet let these winds loose to do harm to the earth," warns one of the angels. The message is clear: If God weren't restraining evil by His merciful power, the world couldn't survive at all.

God has ordered His angels to hold back the worst of the strife. Why? I'm not sure of all of God's purposes. But I'm sure He loves us and has mercy on us. He surely doesn't desire that we suffer. I'm sure He wants all people to have a chance to follow and serve Him before this earth and its societies self-destruct.

The Incarnate God

Here is one more way that God was in evidence in the midst of the September 11 tragedy: He made Himself visible in the goodness of human beings. Picture these scenes with me:

- Police and firemen (including their chaplain) are called into a dangerously infirm tower of the World Trade Center. They don't shirk their duty: there are lives to save. These rescuers die as the towers collapse, but not before they are successful in getting hundreds of other people to safety outside.
- A passenger phones his wife secretly from the plane as it is being hijacked. He tells of a plan by courageous passengers to take the plane from the hijackers before they can do any harm. The result is the plane crashing to the earth, with all the passengers lost. But the building the terrorists intended to hit— perhaps the White House—is saved.
- Day after day hundreds of workers comb the wreckage of the building, first in search of survivors, then in search of remains that at least bring closure to a few grieving families.

• Millions of people hear of the tragedy and respond. A few leave jobs and journey to New York to assist the rescue effort. Many more give blood or write checks to charities that promise to help survivors.

Some have called these folks heroes. They were. But they were something more: They were doers of godly actions.

Years ago, when Jesus came to earth, He blended, in a way inexplicable to us, all the qualities of God into the body of a man. Jesus' mission was summed up in the name the angel gave Him: "They will call him Immanuel"—which means, "God with us" (Matthew 1:23, NIV). And so it was that Jesus became God among us. God became flesh. He is, if we understand Scripture correctly, still one of us.

We call it, in Christian theology, the Incarnation. *Incarnation* means, literally, "to make something into flesh." In Jesus Christ, Divinity became flesh. Yet even ordinary people can incarnate the qualities of God. When a man picks up a shovel and digs a stranger out of the rubble, he is incarnating God's love of life. When a passenger on an airplane resists an evil terrorist, he is incarnating God's hatred of sin. When an ordinary wage-earner writes a check for a charity in order to help others, he is incarnating God's generosity.

We become, in doing good, incarnations of the lovely qualities of God. It is a disquieting responsibility—and one that we ought not to take lightly.

Not long ago I heard a group of children singing this lovely chorus:

We are His hands to touch the world around us.
We are His feet to go where He may lead.
We are His eyes, to see the need in others.
We are His voice, to tell of His return.
And we are His love burning in the darkness.
We are His love shining in the night.[3]

"Every good gift and every perfect gift is from above, and comes down from the Father of lights, with whom is no variation or shadow of turning," said James (James 1:17, NJKV). That includes good impulses, good actions, good sacrifices, and even good intentions. It is a circle, you see: We receive God's impulses and then incarnate them in the works of our hands.

Let us not become confused as we think about this by any New-Age teaching about good people becoming little gods. That's not what I mean at all. Such a claim was originally voiced by Satan to Eve. It was a deception then—and it should have been a fairly transparent one—and so it remains to this day when New-Age gurus voice it.

Yet we Christians do not entirely reject the notion that Divinity can somehow become incarnate in us. Paul called it a mystery that you can have "Christ in you, the hope of glory" (Colossians 1:27). There is something of God's qualities incarnated in each good act, each good word, each good intention. Moments when we do good, with no thought of reward and only the relief of the needs of others in mind, is the closest we human beings will ever come (short of heaven) to being like God.

A friend of mine summed up the September 11 terrorist crisis thus: "For all the evil that was dumped on the world, folks tipped the scale by bringing a whole lot of goodness against it. And the goodness was greater than their evil."

The denouement of the story of Joseph provides us with a poignant and unforgettable explanation of what really happens when good and evil collide. Joseph's brothers had finally been unmasked, their perfidy of many years earlier revealed. They had found their once-enslaved brother Joseph a mighty ruler of a nation on whose resources they were dependent for life. And he knew who they were. They were terrified and begged for their lives. "You intended to harm me," says Joseph, "but God intended it for good to accomplish what is now being done" (Genesis 50:20, NIV).

God has the amazing ability to transform evil into good. It may be hard to understand what good can come from tragedy. I'm sure that some of the people who lost loved ones in those fiery crashes are doubting that the world will ever look good again.

But in at least one place—in the mobilization of good people against an act of Satan—we have seen it happen. Satan and a few of his followers intended to do evil. But the responses of good people have tipped the scales. There was, as odd as it may sound, more serious goodness in the world on September 12, 2001, than there had been on September 10.

---

1. *Thus Spake Zarathustra* (written 1883-1885).

2. I am indebted to the writer of a widely-circulated email, who didn't identify him or herself, for these calculations.

3. "We Are His Hands," ©1986 by Jeff Wood.

CHAPTER 2

WHY GOD LET IT HAPPEN

Let us pause for a parenthesis at the beginning of this chapter. I ask you to attend to me carefully because I have a warning for you.

Whenever we speak of the "whys" of God, we're treading on dangerous ground. When it comes to God's thoughts and actions (or God's seeming inaction), only God knows for sure. All we can do (and that with a great measure of humility) is try to piece together a humble, and certainly partial, understanding of God's "whys" from what He has revealed to us.

This is not the last time in the course of our spiritual analysis of September 11, 2001, and its aftermath that we will have to take such an attitude. Let us admit up front that there is much about God that we don't know—it will save us from overconfidence on one hand and disappointment on the other.

Sometimes believers don't want to hear that. They want to know with certainty everything God is doing, thinking, and planning, as though we humans could have a spy in each meeting of heaven's board of directors. But there are hundreds of questions that we'll never get clear answers to short of our own arrival in heaven—and hundreds more for which I suspect our answers constitute only the best understanding we intellectually limited human beings can grasp. Remember, when we talk about God, we're dealing with infinity: infinite wisdom, infinite goodness, infinite knowledge, infinite power. Human beings really can't get very far in understanding infinity; and viewed in that light, it is amazing to me that we can understand anything at all about the immortal, invisible, all-wise God of the universe.

And, as I already said, what we know is only those things that He chose to reveal to us through "holy men of God" who "spoke as they were moved by the Holy Spirit" (2 Peter 1:21, RSV). If you think about it, our limited ability to understand the infinite should have been the first clue that we couldn't "be like God" (Genesis 3:5, RSV), as the serpent promised in Eden. It is an amazing sign of God's special regard for us that He has given us even as much knowledge of Godself as He has done, and that regard softens my disappointment and frustration at knowing so little.

Yet we constantly push in that direction: The more words we think we are required to say about God, the more ideas about Him we may generate—frequently crossing the boundary of revelation into speculation. The word we use to describe our human tendency to want to know more about God's motives and actions than He has revealed to us is *presumptuous,* and it refers to a kind of arrogant overreaching into realms we don't—and aren't intended to—understand.

Fortunately, some things God has made perfectly clear, so that we aren't left floundering in existential quicksand. God has told us a bit about Himself in words and concepts we *can* understand. Although concepts like "Father" and "Son" are metaphors He has borrowed from the biological relationships of our world, He has used these familiar pictures so we can understand better the dynamics of heavenly relationships.

He has also told us just a bit about one of the biggest mysteries of all: how sin could have arisen on the watch of an all-knowing, all-good, all-powerful Divinity.

THE SHAPE OF THE PROBLEM

Theologians have struggled with the problem of sin's origin for centuries. In classical religious philosophy, the attempt to explain it is known as "theodicy"[1]—the question of how a perfectly good God can coexist in the same universe with evil. The problem goes like this: If God is perfectly good, then He mustn't have had the power to keep sin from appearing; or if He is more powerful than sin, then there must be some flaw in His goodness that let sin happen.

You must see that this *is* a perplexing question. And not just a theoretical one. Tragedies—real tragedies, resulting in the death of thousands of people, young and old, and the tears and pain by which those deaths were given expression—force us to consider it not as a philosophical puzzle, but as a question that gnaws at the very fabric of our existence. Do tragedies like the one that happened at the World Trade Center show God deficient in either power or goodness?

The Scriptures leave no doubt of God's infinite power.

I once read a book by a physicist who listed all the scientific reasons why there couldn't be a God. Principles of physics, he said, make it impossible for there to be anything else in the universe except the laws of cause and effect. Science, he insisted, can explain all the complexities of the universe.

But he didn't understand who God is. That no matter how big the universe, God is bigger. No matter how all-encompassing the scientific principle, God goes beyond it, for He invented the principles and defined them. *By definition,* God is always more powerful than any force in the universe. God is the first cause behind all things that happen. Jeremiah identifies God as

> he who appoints the sun to shine by day,
> who decrees the moon and stars to shine by night,
> who stirs up the sea so that its waves roar (Jeremiah 31:35,
> NIV).

The vastness of such power is beyond our comprehension—and yet sun, moon, stars, and seas are only a sample of His power. God is God from the largest nebula to the smallest quark, and just because we cannot imagine Him that large and powerful, just because we do not see Him in all His glory all the time, we still cannot deny His supremacy over the whole universe.

Nor is His power limited to the spiritual realm. "His eyes watch the nations," insists the psalmist (Psalm 66:7, NIV). In spite of the apparent autonomy of our political processes or the randomness of political disarray (such as we see in Afghanistan or the Middle East), God claims to have some measure of control even in the chaotic arena of human choice. "The authorities that exist have been established by God," wrote Paul, for "there is no authority except that which God has established" (Romans 13:1, NIV). While we doubt that God approves of any repressive regime, we can be quite sure that His power is at work in the rise and fall of governments.

God is, by definition, the mightiest Force in the universe. Name anything, and God is stronger. Picture anything, and God is larger. Listen to any human leader, and he is only a minor functionary compared to God. God is, as one of my favorite hymns says, the "Immortal, invisible, God only wise."

At the same time, the Scriptures do not allow us to entertain doubts of God's goodness. Two of Scripture's most God-connected commentators agree. Very early in His relationship to human beings, God identifies Himself to Moses (to whom He entrusted the Ten Commandments) as "the compassionate and gracious God, slow to anger, abounding in love and faithfulness" (Exodus 34:6, NIV). David, who God describes as "a man after my own heart" (Acts 13:22, NIV), is unequivocal: "How great is your goodness!" (Psalm 31:19, NIV).

What makes His goodness even more striking is that it is not limited to those with whom He is particularly pleased. "The LORD is good to *all*," writes David, for as Creator, "he has compassion on all he has made" (Psalm 145:9, NIV, emphasis supplied). Jesus confirms it with an observation that many have found counterintuitive to their preconceptions of God. "He causes his sun to rise on the evil and the good, and sends rain on the righteous and the unrighteous" (Matthew 5:45, NIV). Luke quotes Him in an even more blunt expression of His goodness: "He is kind to the ungrateful and wicked" (Luke 6:35, NIV).

And so we must reject any notion of a flaw in either God's power or His goodness. Says Moses, in his summary statement about his years of intimacy with God, "His works are perfect, and all his ways are just. A faithful God who does no wrong, upright and just is he" (Deuteronomy 32:4, NIV).

Where then did evil come from?

THE RISK

The answer is this: God took a calculated risk.

He took this risk for the sake of friendship. That is to say, God wished to be surrounded by friends—beings somewhat like Himself, beings who could think and reason, choose and decide, create and imagine, rule and give names and shape the world around them. Genesis 1:26 is not talking about physical characteristics when it says, "Let us make man in our image, in our likeness" (NIV); it is not at all clear from Scripture that God even has an appearance, for "God is spirit" (John 4:24, NIV). The passage in Genesis 1 is talking about our common personality traits and talents, for what God's image bestowed was the possibility of wise rulership—a partial creatorship, if you will—over "the fish of the sea and the birds of the air, over the livestock, over all the earth, and over all the creatures that move along the ground" (v. 26, NIV). That is to say, we human beings were created with a miniature portion of God's ability to think and choose and create and shape the world.

Why was such radical freedom necessary?

I had a delightful time with a group of children one afternoon at a science museum. It is one of those museums that is filled with marvelous hands-on displays intended to help children become fascinated with science. The activities were so much fun that my fascination was growing too. I was deeply absorbed in a display about magnetism when I felt a nudge against my leg.

I looked down to see a curious little creature trying to make friends with me.

It was a metal enclosure that came about to my knees, taller than it was wide, with a metal hook hanging from one shoulder. In place of legs, it traveled on three wheels. Its face, such as it was, consisted of a painted smile, two painted eyes, and a camera lens for a nose. Its ears were two speakers.

Then it spoke to me. "Hello," it said in a flat electronic voice. "I am D-19, your electronic friend."

I was having my first encounter with a robot.

I didn't answer, which was just as well, because D-19 didn't seem interested. It pulled away and moved on to another part of the room.

I studied D-19 for a while. Although it moved under its own power, it didn't seem to have much sense of purpose. It wandered until it encountered an obstacle—as often a table leg as a human being—and repeated its recorded sentence. It could also use its "arm" to pick up a ring from a hook and take it to another hook—interesting, but of limited utility.

As cute as D-19 was, I never for a moment assumed that it was making intelligent choices. Its "brain" was an electronic circuit that could direct its machinery to do a few simple activities for the amusement of museum-goers. Detecting objects with its electronic eye triggered one of several programmed responses. One could hardly call what D-19 did "thinking."

Being able to think and make choices—whether the right choice or the wrong choice—is one of the marks of being human. It is one of the qualities we inherited from God when He created us in His own image.

And any creature—no matter the complexity—that cannot make free choices might as well be D-19.

One author explains it this way:

> God might have created man without the power to transgress His law; He might have withheld the hand of Adam from touching the forbidden fruit; but in that case man would have been, not a free moral agent, but a mere automaton. Without freedom of choice, his obedience would not have been voluntary, but forced.[2]

The price of true friendship with free creatures was creating beings who could choose for or against His wise advice. He had calculated that beings made in His image, given freedom to choose, would naturally choose God's way. Wouldn't it be obvious to any thinking creature that a good Creator would be preferable to any other option, no matter how beguiling?

There are two groups of such beings in the universe. One we know very well: human beings. The other—the angels—we know at least a little about from the Bible. It was in the angels—more precisely, with the chief of all angels—that sin first germinated.

The story of the origin of sin in the universe is found in Ezekiel 28. It is the story of an angel who was highly favored by God, one who was created for the purpose of being God's special associate. "With an anointed guardian cherub I placed you; you were on the holy mountain of God; in the midst of the stones of fire you walked. You were blameless in your ways from the day you were created, till iniquity was found in you." What was that original iniquity? "Your heart was proud because of your beauty; you corrupted your wisdom for the sake of your splendor" (Ezekiel 28:14, 15, 17, RSV).

It seems amazing to us that pride could grow in the heart of one who, though created perfect, was in the presence of his Creator. But the possibility of such a rebellion seems to be the calculated risk God was willing to take to avoid ending up with a planet full of robots. It could have gone either way. Everyone could have chosen wisely and properly, and we'd now be living in a universe of heavenly bliss. Instead, a chief angel gathered followers, and then gathered us human beings into the same mess he was in. He, too, wanted companionship.

One Bad Apple

"All it takes," my mother used to say, "is one bad apple to spoil the rest."

What I had on my hands was one bad apple.

I was speaking to a class of fourth graders one afternoon. It had begun calmly enough. Most seemed to enjoy the story I was telling them.

Except one lad.

From where I was standing, I couldn't even see what deviltry he was perpetrating. There was no question about his influence though. Snickers and smirks and whispers and giggles spread around him, like the circular ripples from a stone dropped into a pond.

The teacher had stepped out for a moment while I was speaking, but like most teachers, she had eyes in the back of her head and the ability to see through walls. She returned, went directly to his seat, and with a stern, "Come with me," marched him out of the classroom.

I don't know where they went or what happened to him next. I only know that when he left, the room became quiet again, and I resumed storytelling.

It's as simple as getting rid of that one bad apple.

Or is it?

With this chief angel's choice to think himself as entitled to worship as God Himself is, there entered into a perfect world one bad apple. A disease, if you will, that infected all of God's perfect creation, both the physical world and the spiritual.

It came in the person of this renegade angel, whom the Bible refers to as Satan, or the devil. By whatever name, he was not a comical figure in a red suit with a pitchfork and tail. He had become, according to Scripture, a powerful enemy of all that is good. And while not God's equal, Satan managed to secure a sphere of influence among the creatures God had created.

SPREADING THE INFECTION

My wife and I love gardens. We have visited some beautiful gardens in many places of the world. (Our favorites are Huntington Botanical Gardens in San Marino, California, and Longwood Gardens near Philadelphia.) Little gives me greater joy than a perfect blossom or an elegantly-formed tree. I love to inhale the heady fragrances of lilacs or roses or to see masses of flowers glowing in jewel-like colors in the morning sunshine, leaves healthy and green.

And so I am challenged, when looking at a stunning garden, to imagine how much more beautiful Eden must have been. As beautiful as this world is now, it is nothing compared to what God originally designed it to be. Neither the beauty of the flora and fauna, nor for that matter the human element, is as perfect as God created it to be.

One of the foundational facts of Christian theology is that this earth started out perfect. Flawless, like God Himself. Then sin entered the world—sin as both a spiritual concept and a physical transformation. The earth was marred spiritually, as well as in its very substance, for this change marked the beginning of deterioration and death. This happened because the infection spread outside of God's heaven. In heaven, the matter came to blows. "There was war in heaven. Michael [Jesus] and his angels fought against the dragon [Satan]" (Revelation 12:7, NIV). Some have even suggested that an enigmatic phrase in Revelation 12:4, "His tail swept a third of the stars out of the sky and flung them to the earth" (NIV), is a metaphor for Satan's winning the loyalty of a third of God's angels and taking them and their now-evil influence down to this planet, to test the remaining group of free-choosing creatures God had created. At the time, the biblical record says there were two of them: a husband and a wife.

The story of how sin entered this planet is recorded in Genesis 3. It tells of Satan's going to the creatures that God had created in His own image and placing before them a challenge: "Why do you trust God so much that you unquestioningly do what He says? Don't you have any freedom? Do what *you* want to do," he says, "even if *He* forbids it!" (See verses 1-5.)

The object of temptation was something of little intrinsic importance—merely fruit on a tree. What *was* important was that God had forbidden them to eat it. At Satan's urging, Adam and Eve, the first man and the first woman, made the decision to eat that fruit against God's explicit prohibition.

And that is how Satan's influence came to be right here on this old earth. Satan brought evil to our world, and he has been promoting it ever since. He, and those of us who are influenced by him (as all of us are from time to time), have been responsible for the tears, sadness, and even death suffered by the inhabitants of this blue-green spinning orb.

Here, then, is the question. It is one that I have asked, and has been asked of me, many times.

Why didn't God simply get rid of that one bad apple?

The moment a bit of evil appeared in Satan (the Bible says it was the result of jealousy and pride), why couldn't God have destroyed him—made him and his rebellious influence simply disappear? Surely God knew what would happen if He did not. Surely He knew that because of Satan, there would arise Hitler, Idi Amin, Stalin, Sadaam

Hussein, and a host of other tyrants responsible for the suffering of millions. Surely He knew that letting that evil one loose on the earth would lead to cancer and AIDS, to depression and loneliness, to birth defects, drug addiction, car accidents, and divorces. Surely He knew that the end result of letting Satan live and practice his evil arts would be an earth full of misery.

So I ask you: Was it really quite fair of God to stick *us* with these problems, when He could quite easily have zapped Satan out of existence?

THE CASE AGAINST ZAPPING

A skeptic once put it to me in this way: "You say God is good. Why would a good God grant His creatures the freedom to kill, murder, thieve, hate, and destroy?"

It's a good question, isn't it? But allow me one question in return.

Would you want a God who refused to give His creatures the freedom to make choices—even if those choices are wrong?

I said earlier that evil is like a disease. That is not entirely accurate. Like a disease, it has spread and infected the earth. But unlike a disease, evil involves a decision. You and I must make decisions about whether to do good or evil, just as our first human father and mother did.

Not long ago we heard that on some farms in Europe a dreaded disease was found in many of the livestock. The authorities didn't want the disease to spread and infect livestock everywhere. So without mercy, they killed and burned the livestock in order to stop the disease from spreading.

And people have often wondered, Why didn't God do that with Satan? Once He detected the germ of pride, of sin, in him, why not just get rid of him and never expose anyone else?

Ah, but God's created creatures—both human and angelic—are not herds of livestock. Don't forget: We were created to be like God. We were created with the ability to look at a situation, to analyze it, to try to understand it. We were given the ability to make free choices, just as God Himself can do. On the point of freedom, we were as much like God as God could make us.

And so when Satan came up with another way of looking at things—when he said, "God is unfair. God is not telling you the whole truth. It is my way that is best, not God's. Follow me instead," what could God do? If this angel, whom Isaiah calls Lucifer, should just suddenly disappear in a flash of lightning and smoke, people might come to this conclusion: "Lucifer tried to tell us about another choice we could make, but God was such a tyrant that He wouldn't let him. If we don't want to be destroyed, then we had better agree with God in everything. So don't exercise your free will. Don't think any new thoughts or anything different from God."

Suddenly people would have lost all their free choice! What could God do? He had to let the old devil present his case to His free people, to see if their freedom would stand up to a choice of loyalty.

And as you recall, our ancestors, the first human beings, made the wrong choice. They chose to disobey God, and so, as Paul says in Romans 5:12, "sin came into the world through one man and death through sin" (RSV).

The Freedom Paradox

The destruction in New York and Washington, D.C., said President George W. Bush, was an act of war. You have now seen that God, too, is in a war. The wars we fight on this earth are just reflections of those in the spiritual realm. Satan is a terrorist, who with his angels is waging a spiritual campaign that makes even our worst battles seem small. That war is invisible to us, but it is happening. And the stakes are high. What is at stake in this war is the rulership of God over the universe.

We human beings have been enlisted in this war. Each one—God and Satan—wants to win our allegiance. Each makes his case. Satan tries to describe God as a tyrant. To make his case, he stirs our selfish desires and tries to enlist our anger. God assures us that Satan is a liar and a destroyer. He made His case by displaying utter unselfishness—giving His Son to die for us on the cross.

Yet in order to make sure that the choice we make is our own, God has granted us a terrifying freedom: the freedom to choose between good and evil. Only in this way can God avoid the accusation that He coerces us by His superior power. The paradox is that such freedom means we can choose to commit horrible sins.

And now we come to the heart of the matter, as it affects the events of September 11, 2001. Should it be at all surprising, then, that some human beings would let Satan influence them to choose to do horrible things—like flying airplanes into buildings full of people? Should it surprise us that Satan could induce people to mail letters filled with dangerous microbes through the mail to innocent and unsuspecting people? Should it surprise us that some have chosen to be so evil that they don't care whether they are killing adults or children? To a truly evil person, under the influence of a truly evil and powerful ex-angel, the entire world is an enemy. Should it surprise us that the terrorists committed suicide in their attempt? Evil is nothing if not self-destructive.

WHY ALL THIS STRUGGLE?

"All right," you might say, "I'll accept your argument that God could not have taken away humankind's freedom of choice without turning us into robots. But frankly, at this point in my life, I know *quite* enough about evil. Why doesn't God do more to help us *now?* Why should we have to face these same horrible problems—war, genocide, ethnic cleansing, mass murders, terrorism—again and again and again?"

What you really are asking is why God doesn't zap evil out of our world in the same way that we would have liked him to zap Satan out of existence. Yet even with the most evil people, God allows a choice.

A documentary program not long ago interviewed a much-publicized con-artist, who had bilked hundreds of people out of millions of dollars. His crimes were despicable, and ultimately he was caught. He was caught not because he'd made a flaw—he was too cunning for that—but because his conscience had begun to bother him. At the last moment, the immorality of his continuing dishonesty began (quite unexpectedly) to make him unhappy.

It is never too late for human beings to make a choice between good and evil. That's why God doesn't close the door on anyone until He knows the chances for the right choice are exhausted.

Yes, there are victims of such free choices. And I'm not able to explain why some died and some escaped; why some stayed home from the World Trade Center while others were at work. But I do know this: Even in the worst tragedies—even in those events that leave us suffering and struggling—God is working on us.

Not long ago, I heard a newsman interviewing an award-winning athlete. The athlete described the long hours of preparation he'd put into his sport—as many as ten hours of intense training a day, every day of the year; a special diet; a restricted regimen of rest and recreation.

"But you were head and shoulders above the competition," the newsman exclaimed. "Couldn't you have won without so much struggle?"

"Yes, I think I could have," the athlete responded. "But without that struggle, I would not have appreciated the win quite so much."

I told you above that without freedom, one cannot be fully human. The corollary is that without struggle and suffering, one cannot develop the character we need to face Satan's temptations.

I once met a man whose mother had never allowed him to make a mistake. She feared that he might put himself in danger. So she kept him at home, never allowing him the freedom to become educated or to marry. He never made a mistake—but he had no character either. He never faced a challenge, and so he grew into a dull man who lived a dull life, lacking courage, ambition, and interests. Late in his life, when his mother died, it became clear what a crippling handicap was his inexperience at making his own decisions. He died a helpless old fool.

Those who never struggle will never learn. Those who never work will never develop strength. Those who never stretch themselves will never reach a higher mark.

And those who never grapple with sin will never conquer it.

EARNING TRUST

Once upon a time, a CEO of a company had a staff of workers who loved him, a board of directors that trusted him, and a popular assistant who helped him with the details of running things.

It so happened that the assistant, for selfish reasons, began furtively to suggest to others that the CEO was cheating the company out of money.

It was a devastating blow to a leader who had always tried to be honest and upright. Even more devastating was the realization that some among the work force and the company board believed it.

You see, the assistant had not been careless; long before he sowed his lies, he'd prepared the soil. With disarming charm and thoughtful gestures, he'd made friends around the company. And so when he whispered accusations, many believed him. Some even suggested that the board of directors ought to make him the company CEO—an idea that may have been at the bottom of the accusation in the first place.

Now, the CEO could have fired the assistant the moment he began his campaign of insinuation. But he realized that if he removed his accuser, whatever trust remained among his people would disappear. Even people who believed in the CEO might think, *Perhaps he does have something to hide. He fires those who disagree with him.* People work poorly for a leader they don't trust; morale would plummet and so would productivity.

And the company CEO made the odd decision to allow his assistant to continue working. *Sooner or later,* he reasoned, *a man like this will show his true colors. His dishonesty will become apparent. And when people find out what he is like, it will become clear to all that they have been deceived.*

And so it happened. The company went through a difficult period of struggle and sadness. But in the end, everyone realized the accuser's perfidy, and he left the company.

As for the CEO, his position in the company was strengthened. People admired him all the more for his patience in letting the situation develop. His future was assured. And his company's future grew even brighter.

Like that CEO, God has chosen to let Satan continue his efforts to win allegiance to himself. Had He not, neither angels nor humankind could ever have been certain that God had given His opponent a fair chance to prove his point.

Unlike that story, the stakes for us are universal and eternal. We have, sadly, been caught in the middle.

But it will not always be so. In the end, Satan will lose. It will be clear to all that God can be trusted, and people will live as God originally intended. " 'The dwelling of God [will be] with men, and he will live with them. They will be his people, and God himself will be with them and be their God. He will wipe every tear from their eyes. There will be no more death or mourning or crying or pain, for the old order of things has passed away' " (Revelation 21:3, 4, NIV).

An Assisted Struggle

I hope that I have convinced you that there are reasons why sin seems to be running rampant in our world. I may have left you with the impression that we don't have much of a chance against the devil. Nothing can be further from the truth. And this is the reason: We are not left alone to fight against sin.

Just because Satan has gained a foothold on our planet doesn't mean that God has ceased to assist us. He puts incredible strength on our side.

From the very beginning, God had a plan to rescue us from Satan. The plan came together in Jesus Christ. Through a perfect life, an unmerited death, and a glorious resurrection, Jesus showed us that God is on our side—and always will be. Jesus showed that Satan can be overcome—and He promised that we too can overcome him.

Many Christians can testify that it is true. They can tell you of glorious answers to prayer, of supernatural help to overcome bad habits, of spiritual peace in times of grief or pain, of growth in personal understanding and character.

And so we who trust God are left with no doubt as to how this conflict between good and evil will play out. His presence and help, when we seek Him in prayer, has given us reason for confidence in Him.

And that is why we are so certain that in the end, there will no longer exist even a single terrorist in all of God's universe.

---

1. After *Théodicé,* a work by seventeenth-century philosopher Baron Gottfried Wilhelm von Leibnitz.

2. Ellen G. White, *Patriarchs and Prophets* (Hagerstown, Md.: Review and Herald, 1958) p. 49.

FINDING PEACE AGAIN

Even sitting back in an overstuffed easy chair, she was as tense as a statue. As if every muscle were a piano wire. She twisted the handkerchief she was holding in her hands, pausing only to press it to her eyes. "Ever since this happened," she said, "I just can't relax. I'm worried all the time." She leaned forward and looked into my eyes. "My children live in New York," she said. My face, too, tightened with concern. "Not the city, Pastor," she added. "Just the state. Buffalo. But I just keep thinking, what if something happens to them?"

"But Irene," I wanted to interrupt, "Buffalo is almost as far from New York City as Ohio is! They're in no more danger than you are!" I didn't say it, though. The answer to her anxiety wasn't a geography lesson. She wasn't really talking about facts, but feelings. Deep, wrenching anxiety that kept her awake at night and drained her energy.

"I've always lived a peaceful life," she said. I glanced around her perfectly tidy living room: family pictures (some sepia with age), hand-crocheted antimacassars gracing each upholstered chair, a vase of her home-grown roses on the coffee table. The picture of domestic peace and security. Not a sign, not the slightest hint, of terror in this warm and lovely place. "And now this has to happen." She sighed deeply and cast a disdainful look at the console television set across the room, as though the appliance itself deserved the blame for what it had shown her: a vivid, full color, live-action picture of a Boeing 767 jet-propelled airplane slamming into the city's tallest building. She'd seen it happen, live, as she was sipping her morning tea. Since then she'd rarely turned the television off: Even as we spoke, I could see a CNN reporter's talking head mouthing news of Afghanistan, the sound muted but the text of her words scrolling across the bottom of the screen.

"My husband thinks I'm being silly. He just says, 'Irene, get over it. The kids are going to be OK.' But I'm just not sure. I'm not sure of anything anymore. I thought—" She turned both palms up with her fingers outspread in a gesture expressive of both emphasis and frustration. "I thought that we'd *always* be safe from this kind of thing—in the United States at least."

I've met others who've had Irene's reaction. "We thought something like this could never happen," they say. "Now it has, and it feels as if the rug has been yanked out from under us." It is a common human reaction, and the word that we use for it—*insecurity*—doesn't quite begin to convey how it feels when life's fundamental truths suddenly prove false.

For a number of years my wife and I lived in northern California. Earthquakes aren't unexpected in California, but the one that struck San Francisco in 1989 was unusually strong. There were mercifully few casualties; fewer people died in the earthquake than die each day from accidents on California's highways. But while most people don't worry about driving just because traffic accidents happen, many began to worry about earthquakes. Some people had their sense of security about the San Francisco Bay Area permanently shattered. They packed their belongings into a moving van and left. I heard one man explain it this way: "All your life you walk on the ground, and the ground stays where it is supposed to. It is one thing you intuitively know you can *absolutely* count on— the ground will stay put. Wind and water may move, but not the ground. And ever since the ground moved, I just can't relax here anymore."

The attack on a major United States city was an earthquake of the spirit. Anthrax-laced mail made a familiar, everyday event seem ominous. The earth moved. People have spent months trying to feel safe again. Even if, by the time you read these words, some of the worst shocks and aftershocks of September 11, 2001 have passed, we'll need to be prepared for other spiritual earthquakes.

How do you find peace after your world has been shaken? There are things you can do to calm an unsettled heart.

1. Put Life Back Into Perspective

Sometimes when people feel as Irene did, they think their feelings are out of their control. That the events "out there" dictate the reaction "in here"—in their hearts and minds. Over and over again, though, people have shown that they can affect their emotional reactions by the thoughts they think.

You start by putting your life into perspective.

For one thing, this disaster isn't all of life. It is just one event. You had a happy and peaceful life before it happened. All evidences are that you may well have many years of happy, peaceful life afterward too.

Rather than just saying this to Irene, though, I simply asked her questions about her life. About raising her children in this comfortable and happy house. About her marriage to a good husband. About the pictures on the mantelpiece. About the many years she'd been part of our church family and all the wonderful friends she has there. We even talked about her roses and about the little herb garden I could see from the living-room window from which she'd harvested the spearmint that flavored the tea we were drinking. I asked her about her family and learned that children and grandchildren were coming for her birthday.

What I wanted Irene to understand was that there was a whole lot more to her life than a horrible terrorist strike 500 miles away. The threat of terrorism needn't be a big part of her life at all. For the moment, the threat has been contained. Those particular terrorists are dead. Airport security has been tightened. New York City is far away. Though indeed some Americans have been killed by terrorists, the vast majority of us will be affected not at all. We are in less danger from terrorists than we are of dying of heart attacks or car accidents. And the vast majority of us will make it through this day of life without suffering even those more common tragedies.

Furthermore, at the moment, Irene and I are sitting in a cozy living room sipping mint tea. We can put all of the rest of it out of our minds. We can live in this moment. We can thank God for comfort, for peace, for friendship.

Why take all the pain of a possible future tragedy on our hearts before it happens? The things we most greatly fear usually don't happen. But think of all the time we might spend suffering over them!

I was sitting by the hospital bed of a man who'd been diagnosed with a curable disease. There was a possibility that it could become worse, but only a slight one. Yet he persisted in talking to me about his will and his funeral! "I don't think you're in that much danger," I said.

"Listen, Pastor," he said. "You never know what might happen. I'm just being realistic."

I've noticed that people who claim to be "just realistic" are very often highly pessimistic. They adjust their minds to the worst possibilities and then live as though the worst were actually happening to them. There is a possibility that you will get a terminal illness, of course. There is also a possibility that you might lose your job. There is even a possibility that your wife may leave you for another man. And there is a possibility that a terrorist may strike your city, and you'll be in the path. These are at least possibilities.

But a realistic assessment of your life would tell you that much more has gone right than has gone wrong. A realistic assessment would take into account that you've lived for decades without terminal illness! You've had to change jobs only twice in your life, and each time you found another! Your marriage, though it may not be perfect, is stable! And you've lived your whole life without ever even knowing a terrorist, much less being attacked by one! In most of life, the very worst possibility is one of the least likely possibilities.

My friend in the hospital bed was unconvinced. He was only preparing himself by anticipating the worst scenario, he said, in case it happens. "If the worst happens, then I won't be surprised. If it doesn't happen, then I can still feel relieved." And yet his living in fear of the worst was causing him great emotional pain and might even have contributed to the worsening of his illness. I wondered why he didn't do exactly the opposite: prepare himself for a good outcome. And then, I suggested, he could still feel disappointed should it turn out bad! I reminded him of Julius Caesar's words in Shakespeare's play: "Cowards die many times before their deaths; The valiant never taste of death but once."[1]

"I'm just being realistic," he said.

"If that's realistic," I told him, "then I wish you'd be a little out of touch with reality!" By the thoughts he'd chosen, he'd thrown his entire life out of perspective.

There is much more to your life than the traumatic events that are robbing your peace at this moment. You had a good life before they happened, and you will be happy again. The Lord has provided many blessings. Put your life back into perspective.

"But what if the worst happens? Then what?" Then we face the worst. Then we cope with it, just as we'd cope with any crisis: a heart attack, a car accident, the death of a friend. Then we place our faith in the "God of all comfort, who comforts us in all our affliction, so that we may be able to comfort those who are in any affliction, with the comfort with which we ourselves are comforted by God" (2 Corinthians 1:3, 4, RSV).

2. TAKE CARE OF YOURSELF

"Ever since the disaster, I haven't been eating or sleeping well," Irene told me. "Why not?" I asked. "Well, I've been staying up late to watch the news; then I can't sleep. And I just haven't felt like eating. I've lost a sense of my normal routine."

Common sense says that when people don't sleep and eat well, not only will they feel physically less well, but their emotional durability will diminish. "Irene," I said, "these are things you can choose to do. You can try to eat. You can turn off the television set and go to bed." I suggested that the more quickly she get back to her normal routine, the better she would feel.

In the twenty-third psalm, the terror of walking "through the valley of the shadow of death" is balanced by a list of take-care-of-yourself messages. The Lord "makes me lie down in green pastures," the psalmist says. "He leads me beside still waters; he restores my soul. He leads me in paths of righteousness for his name's sake" (RSV). His presence supplies comfort. Even the need of nourishment is addressed, for even when enemies threaten, the Lord prepares a table of food for me, anoints me with perfumed oil (the ancient equivalent of a fragrant lotion), and fills for me a bottomless cup of spearmint tea!

These are, I believe, the Lord's recommendations for people who are fearful and afraid. You have the Lord's permission to take care of yourself, even to pamper yourself! In the midst of a crisis is not a time to be hard on ourselves, but a time to enjoy the Lord's best, most comforting gifts.

Part of taking care of yourself is guiding and guarding your thoughts. A friend of mine calls this "mental hygiene"—taking the same care to keep your thoughts healthy as you would to keep your body healthy.

Shortly after September 11, 2001, my wife and I had to attend a meeting near Baltimore. One morning we ate breakfast in the cafe in the hotel lobby. There was a television set in the middle of the lobby playing CNN Headline News. A young woman came in, snatched a cup of coffee, and then sat down in a chair directly in front of the television set. For almost an hour she sat there, bolt upright, cradling her drink and staring at the screen. She hardly blinked or moved a muscle. She hung on every redundant detail of the news. Her mouth was literally hanging open. She was transfixed.

As I watched her, I began to wonder whether it is necessarily wise or healthy for people to so saturate their minds in tragic events that they lose perspective on the rest of life. And shouldn't that be especially true of people who believe that God is in control?

The instant news of our age has had deleterious effects on our ability to cope with traumatic events. I once heard an interview with an elderly woman about her memories of World War I. "Were you worried when you heard about huge battles with many losses?" she was asked. "You must remember," she replied, "that by the time we heard bad news, it could be several weeks in the past. Since it hadn't affected us yet, we figured we could cope with it." That's quite unlike how things are now. Today, a helicopter with a live TV camera feeds a horrible event live into millions of homes as it happens. We watch the buildings fall. We see the very letters that had anthrax in them, almost the moment they are discovered. The most dramatic footage is replayed, dozens of times in an hour, on several networks simultaneously.

And even when no news is happening, the newscasters don't let us get back to ordinary life: They interview experts or speculate about implications or review what has recently happened or tune in to some politician's news conference about what happened. The gravity or excitement in the reporter's voice makes us think we have to give each new detail great weight. Sometimes it feels like being on an emotional roller coaster. Around each bend there's a new fear, a new problem, a new risk. We end up being subjected to tragedy over and over and over again. It is no wonder that people thousands of miles away from the situation—people who've never even visited New York City or the Pentagon—find themselves emotionally exhausted by it!

At times people seem do things that cultivate fear in themselves. They immerse themselves in the news, read about the events, write of them, and talk of them. A friend emailed me in great distress about the political implications of the 9/11 terrorism, worrying what the President would do, wondering what would happen in Afghanistan, and whether Democrats or Republicans had the right approach. The questions weighed heavily on his mind. He had read extensively about the matter. Yet he was sickening himself about details over which he had no control. His fixation showed that he was practicing poor mental hygiene.

Even religion can be misused. I know Christians who since September 11, 2001, have become focused on searching the prophecies of Daniel and Revelation to try to place the terrorism on a prophetic timeline. Yet they seem to find little comfort in it. Their quest is for a bit of esoteric information that might put them one step ahead of everyone else. Yet they seem to become increasingly tense the more they study.

That, too, is poor mental hygiene. For whether or not these events are signs that Jesus is coming very soon, I do know one thing for sure: If this is the time of the end, God will take care of it. If this is the time of the end, God will take care of you—whether or not you know the prophetic timeline. Figuring out what this crisis portends for planet Earth is one you can safely trust to God's wise management.

The end of time and Jesus' coming a second time are supposed to be a joy. If they are a source of great and terrible anxiety to you, if you are watching the news and lying awake at night, then they have become a burden to you, and it is time to let Jesus take that burden.

So there were things Irene could do to calm her fears. Healing from any difficult event doesn't happen quickly. Life is not a sprint, but a marathon, and in a marathon you try to conserve your energy. You take care of yourself. You slow down when you need to—and even stop and rest when you can't go any farther. In distressing times it is especially important to walk in green pastures, lie down by still waters, and let the Lord restore your soul.

3. Turn to the Lord for Comfort

"The Lord is my shepherd, I shall not want." Especially when life is distressing we must remind ourselves that we are under the care of a generous and loving Lord. And yet in hard times, we may fail to turn to Him. Perhaps we become preoccupied and begin to focus on our own insecurity. Perhaps we just get too busy worrying to ask God for comfort!

Let's start with prayer. Prayer is nothing more than telling God what's on your mind. It is "the opening of the heart to God as to a friend."[2] Millions of people can testify that peace has come over them when they asked God to comfort them in times of difficulty.

Years and years ago I first read the following description of prayer. I wish I could frame it and hang it in the heart of every troubled person.

> Keep your wants, your joys, your sorrows, your cares, and your fears before God. You cannot burden Him; you cannot weary Him. He who numbers the hairs of your head is not indifferent to the wants of His children. "The Lord is very pitiful, and of tender mercy." James 5:11. His heart of love is touched by our sorrows and even by our utterances of them. Take to Him everything that perplexes the mind. Nothing is too great for Him to bear, for He holds up worlds, He rules over all the affairs of the universe. Nothing that in any way concerns our peace is too small for Him to notice. There is no chapter in our experience too dark for Him to read; there is no perplexity too difficult for Him to unravel. No calamity can befall the least of His children, no anxiety harass the soul, no joy cheer, no sincere prayer escape the

lips, of which our heavenly Father is unobservant, or in which He takes no immediate interest. "He healeth the broken in heart, and bindeth up their wounds." Psalm 147:3. The relations between God and each soul are as distinct and full as though there were not another soul upon the earth to share His watchcare, not another soul for whom He gave His beloved Son.[3]

Yet while the Lord wants us to pray for our own needs, there is also the danger that, done wrongly, praying for oneself can be counterproductive. "Oh Lord," we pray, "You know how troubled I am. I just worry all the time. I'm in such pain. I'm not happy. I don't know what I'm going to do." And on and on and on. Over and over and over.

Some folks list their complaints to the Lord for hours! Now, all of those complaints may well be true. And our Lord surely won't tire of hearing them. But here's the problem: In just a few short sentences you have managed to repeat all your problems and shortcomings so many times, to articulate them so clearly, that they actually become burned into your mind even more than they were before!

One day on the way to work, a man slipped and slightly twisted his ankle. He managed to get to work anyway and was greeted as he came in the door by his colleagues with, "Hey, Tom. How are you today?" *I think I'll be honest for once,* he thought. "I'm terrible, thanks," he said. "Twisted my ankle on the way to the office. Hurts something awful." Everyone was very sympathetic. Folks ran errands for him like they never had before. The attention went on for several days until his ankle was better. *This honesty thing works,* he thought. So the next week when they asked him how he was, he said, "I've got a stomach ache today, and the arthritis in my hand is hurting." Folks were again sympathetic, but not as much as before. That's when he was almost relieved when he fell down the stairs one morning and broke his wrist. Over the next few months he always had some new health complaint. Hardly a conversation passed that he didn't manage to slip in another ailment. When he ran out of physical ailments he talked about his depression and inability to sleep. The more he noted his health deficiencies, the more he seemed to find! While people seemed to be still concerned, he noticed they weren't spending as long worrying about him as they once had. One day he overheard one employee say to another, "You'll have to see Tom about that. You know Tom, don't you? The man who's always complaining."

The more we repeat something—even if it is something we say we'd like to be rid of—the better we learn it! The more we say it—even if it is something we'd like to change—the more deeply it becomes our identity! After a while the prayer itself subtly reinforces the very things we say we want God to take away! That we bring the same complaints back over and over and over again shows that we're not looking for evidence that the Lord is doing anything at all about them!

When Irene told me about her cares and worries, I asked her, "Irene, have you prayed?"

"Oh, yes," she said. "Constantly."

"For what?" I asked.

"Mostly for myself and my family," she admitted.

I suggested to Irene that one strategy for healing her troubled heart would be to pray her prayers differently. I suggested that she cast her thoughts out to the many people more directly affected by September 11 than she was. "But I don't know any of them," she protested. Fortunately, you don't need to know their names to pray for them. All you have to do is picture them in your mind and ask God to lend His grace. Some suggestions:

- Pray for the victims, that God will comfort those left to mourn, as well as those injured, hurt, and in pain.
- Pray for those engaged in recovery.

- Pray that the tragedy will give the Lord an opening in hearts that might otherwise, in less unsettled times, be closed to Him.
- Pray for our world leaders, that God will guide them in perplexing problems.
- Pray for all the innocent people affected by war.
- Pray (and this is surely hard) for the perpetrators of the crime. Yet this is something that Jesus explicitly asked His followers to do (see Matthew 5:44).

And here are some prayers that we can safely pray for ourselves at any time:

- Pray for unselfishness, that our own fears and anxious thoughts won't drown out concern for others.
- Pray that God would show us how He would have us reach outside our own sphere of interest and help Him touch others' lives.
- Pray that God's will be done in your life and that you will accept it—whether or not you particularly like what He's doing!
- Pray that the Lord will give you the faith to believe that He is responding to our prayers—even if we don't always see *how* He's responding.

There is another aspect of prayer that many pray-ers need to learn. It is that prayer is not simply talking, but listening. Prayer should be the communication between friends. What kind of friendship would you have if your friend never listened?

"But God never says anything to me!" you protest. If you are listening for God to speak to you in words, you may not hear anything. God's speaking to people in an audible voice seems the exception rather than the rule.

Perhaps we need to learn to listen differently.

Composer John Cage is considered by some to be one of the most important composers of the twentieth century. Of all that he composed, he is best remembered for a piece called "4 minutes 33 seconds." When it was first performed in 1952 in Woodstock, New York, it caused a great sensation. Pianist David Tudor sat down at the piano and placed on the music stand a score, marked with measures but no notes. He signaled the beginning of the piece by closing the piano lid. Then for the next four minutes and thirty-three seconds, Tudor sat watching a stopwatch and periodically turning pages of the blank musical score. At the end he stood and bowed. He had "played" four minutes and thirty-three seconds of silence.

Some thought it was a practical joke. Others were insulted. But Cage intended neither to shock nor to make people laugh, but simply to make people listen. One of the reasons the "performance" was so memorable was that the pianist's silence when they expected him to produce sound had made them nervously sensitive to any sound. Witnesses' accounts say that in the first part of the piece, those who were listening became exquisitely aware of the sound of the wind in the trees; in the second part, of raindrops on the roof.

Cage always affirmed that it was his most important work. "I listen to it every day,"[4] he said.

Prayer, we are well schooled to believe, is speaking. Verbalizing. Talking to God. But the thoughtful pray-ers of the Bible knew that in prayer, God also speaks. "Speak, LORD, for your servant is listening," said Samuel (1 Samuel 3:9, NIV). What would happen if while praying, while kneeling, while connected to God, we ceased our one-sided chatter, quieted our minds, and began to listen? We might be surprised what we'd hear.

These are the things most prayer listeners receive:

- *We receive impressions from God.* These impressions may be emotions (a sudden unexplained comfort) or ideas (a thought that seems to gather up scattered fears and make them less scary).
- *We receive reminders of what the Scriptures have already told us.* I believe very strongly that much of the divine communica-

tion we need has already been given to us in the Bible. People who don't read the Bible but ask for the Lord to answer them are like those who want to know the news but won't pick up the newspaper! The Bible is the source of the words of counsel and comfort that God has for you. When you pray (and you may even do that with a Bible open before you) God makes those words personal. He makes them apply to you.

A friend facing a dangerous operation told me that while praying for peace of mind, God had reminded him of a memory text he'd learned many years before. "For I know the plans I have for you, says the LORD, plans for welfare and not for evil, to give you a future and a hope" (Jeremiah 29:11, RSV). "I've known that text for years," he said. "When I really needed it, the Lord brought it back to my mind and used it to give me reassurance. God has planned for me to have a good future! And it suddenly occurred to me that whether that future was a long one here on this earth, or death and eternal life, I'd be happy either way!"

• *We receive assignments.* Sometimes when I'm praying, or even when I'm just sitting at my desk with my heart open to the Lord's voice, a face or a name will pop into my mind. I call that person and say, "I just felt God wanted me to call you. What's happening in your life right now?" And frequently they'll tell me of a need or problem that I didn't know about, but God did.

In fact, that's how I came to visit Irene!

4. DO GOOD FOR OTHERS

Doing good is recommended throughout the Scriptures—a requirement of the spiritual life. But it was from Isaiah that I learned of its healing power. When people seek God in prayer, some think (and perhaps this was true of my friend Irene) that God asks for introspection and self-denial. In Isaiah's time, people did this by fasting—

abstaining from food until you were weak and felt awful, while sitting on sackcloth and ashes. Through the prophet, God told them that the spiritual service He desired was something else entirely.

> Is not this the fast that I choose: to loose the bonds of wickedness, to undo the thongs of the yoke, to let the oppressed go free, and to break every yoke? Is it not to share your bread with the hungry, and bring the homeless poor into your house; when you see the naked, to cover him, and not to hide yourself from your own flesh? (Isaiah 58:6, 7, RSV).

This is what pleases the Lord: to reach out from yourself and do something for others! But please notice the result that God promises: "Then shall your light break forth like the dawn, and *your healing shall spring up speedily*" (verse 8, RSV, emphasis supplied). If you are seeking inner healing, practice looking outward, at the needs of others, rather than inward. Get out of the house. Visit a shut-in friend. There are many people who could use a kind word. Volunteer (there are hundreds of options). Take food to a local food pantry. Donate blood.

Charitable organizations received millions of dollars after September 11. Ostensibly, people gave to help the victims of the tragedy. But clearly, it did something else; giving healed the givers. It gave them the inner perspective to see life clearly. And I suspect that those who helped others most recovered their spiritual equilibrium most quickly.

5. Practice Thankfulness

There is simply no better way to put life in perspective following a tragedy than to be intentionally thankful. I have often counseled people that to enumerate your blessings to God in prayer is more powerful in healing troubled hearts than to enumerate your problems to Him.

We're constantly putting in orders to God, but how rarely we do an inventory of what He's already given us! Gratitude is how we know that God has answered our prayers. The man who never practices gratitude in a serious way—and I mean, not just perfunctory mutterings, but genuine meditation on his blessings—never receives an answer to a prayer, because he never does an inventory. The reflection—the backward glance that measures progress—is missing. And as a consequence, he doesn't even know what to ask for any longer, and he ends up, like a grumbling child, talking to God about whatever seems to be bothering him at the moment.

I heard once of a couple who gave a sizable contribution to their church in honor of their son, who'd been killed serving in the military. When the announcement of this generous contribution was made in church, another woman turned to her husband and whispered, "Let's give the same amount in honor of our son!"

The husband said, "What are you talking about? Our son wasn't killed!"

She said, "That's just the point, isn't it?"

It is so easy to let the blessings slide by. To blithely move on to the next need, the next goal, the next problem. And completely forget the blessings!

The great American preacher Henry Ward Beecher used a memorable illustration on the value of gratitude:

> If one should give me a dish of sand and tell me there were particles of iron in it, I might look for them with my eyes and search for them with my clumsy fingers, and be unable to detect them; but let me take a magnet and sweep through it and now would it draw to itself the almost invisible particles by the mere power of attraction.
>
> The unthankful heart, like my finger in the sand, discovers no mercies; but let the thankful heart sweep through the

day and as the magnet finds the iron, so it will find, in every hour, some heavenly blessings.[5]

Jesus really had, in many ways, a tragic life. He was born in poverty, conceived, some thought, out of wedlock. His family became refugees; when they did return to their own land, they settled in the unpromising village of Nazareth. He worked as a carpenter until He was about thirty years old. He spent the rest of His life being opposed and threatened and was executed by the age of thirty-three.

So why was Jesus so grateful? Even at the moment that His enemies were plotting to capture Him and one of His friends had betrayed Him, even as He felt the cold hand of death—even then, He took food in His hands and thanked God for it!

That's because in the midst of tragedy, Jesus viewed the ultimate goal of a Christian life with optimism. He didn't always *feel* optimistic. But still He thanked God. Jesus *acted* as though the universe were in good hands, even though He knew He Himself faced imminent tragedy.

In the end all things work together for our good, and that is what we're thankful for. Gratitude makes us focus on the good, when circumstances tempt us to focus on the bad. It makes us focus on the blessings rather than on our disappointments. It helps us focus on possibility and ability rather than on failure and weakness.

In the little town of Enterprise, Alabama, is an odd monument dedicated to (of all things) the Mexican boll weevil. In the last decade of the nineteenth century, that insect invaded the county and virtually destroyed the cotton crop. The community thought all was lost. But because of the weevil, farmers were forced to diversify into other crops, and by 1920 the local farmers were wealthy from growing peanuts. The inscription on the monument says, "In profound appreciation of the boll weevil and what it has done as the herald of prosperity."

God can redeem tragedy. Surely no one is glad for the events of September 11. Yet gratitude helps us see that sometimes life's worst moments were preparation for a new victory. There will never be a shortage of tragedies in life. But grateful people know that blessings will follow. God is more powerful than evil. Even in the face of the very, very worst, we know there is a heaven for those who have been thankful to God through life.

And, when you think about it, what else could heaven be but an eternity of gratitude?

---

1. *Julius Caesar,* Act II, Scene 2.

2. Ellen G. White, *Steps to Christ* (Nampa, Idaho: Pacific Press, 1956), p. 93.

3. White, *Steps to Christ,* p. 100.

4. Duckworth, William, *Talking Music* (New York: Schirmer, 1995) pp. 13-15.

5. *Life Thoughts, gathered from the extemporaneous discourses of Henry Ward Beecher, by one of his congregation* (Boston: Phillips, Samson & Company, 1859), p. 116.

WHAT KIND OF PEOPLE ARE THESE?

Most of the people we see during the course of an average day are people who we can, more or less, understand. We don't know their inner thoughts, of course, but we can communicate with one another. We understand, at least in a general way, one another's hopes and needs and fears and concerns and joys, because they're not that much different from our own.

And yet from time to time we'll encounter someone who puzzles us. Whose motives are dark to us. And that is how many people feel about the September 11, 2001, terrorists. Most of us found no point of empathy with them. How could they kill men, women, and children indiscriminately? What level and quality of malice would make it possible to even imagine such an act—much less carry it out? What could possibly motivate people to go to such an extreme? Why do they seem to hate us?

In short, what kind of person could do such a thing?

There are two answers. The first one is factual and informational. It yields, however, less for our spiritual growth than the second answer, which we'll consider in the next chapter.

The first answer—the easy one—is to say that these terrorists were Muslims.

THE FAITH OF MUHAMMAD

I am a committed Christian; that is, I believe in Jesus Christ as the perfect expression of God's character. I have never been anything but a Christian and never will be. Yet I am about to say some kind things about the Muslim religion.

This is not because I have changed loyalties, but because it is wise to try to be as generous toward the opinions of others as one hopes they are toward yours. This generosity extends, as well, to other religions. Because I wouldn't want non-Christians to do it to Christianity, I can see no advantage in caricaturing the world's other faiths. Nor would caricatures be fair or honest; for even if another religion's truth is not complete, fair-minded people would admit that all faiths contain truths, partial though they may be.

For a number of years, I've watched with some concern as Western reporters covered the actions and activities of people who are identified as Muslims. It is not that the reportage is untrue. Indeed, some horrific things have been done in the name of Allah (the Muslim name for God). But a few evil Muslim newsmakers might have skewed the picture we have.

You may be surprised to learn that Islam is a relative of Christianity.

Most Christians know of the relationship between Judaism and Christianity. The development of Christian churches as a subgroup of Judaism is well documented in the New Testament. (The effort to tear itself loose from the mother religion was among the earliest of Christianity's struggles—a problem Paul discussed in extended passages of several of his letters and in almost the entire book of Galatians.)

The connection between Judaism and Christianity has to do with the ethnic group to whom the Messiah was prophesied and to whom He first came. While Jesus was a new expression of the faith of the Hebrew Scriptures, Christianity had much in common with the Jewish faith. A strong sense of morality and monotheism—the belief in one God—were common to them both. History reports that many quite civilized people—notably the Greeks and Romans—were impressed with these features of Judeo-Christian thought, just as Jews and Christians admired and adopted the Greek language and Roman civilities.

After the Christian era began in earnest, it appeared that monotheism was here to stay. But by half a millennium after Christ, the entire Arabian Peninsula was still peopled by nomadic shepherds and traders whose faith was polytheistic and idolatrous. One of these Arabs was a trader named Muhammad. Born about 570 C.E. and orphaned by the age of six, Muhammad grew into a man of native spiritual sensitivity, accompanied by strong leadership skills. In the course of his trading expeditions, he met Christians and Jews and talked with them about their faith.

Troubled by the questions these conversations raised, he began to meditate in a cave outside of the city of Mecca, in the area that is today Saudi Arabia. There, at the age of forty, he claimed that the archangel Gabriel appeared to him in a vision and appointed him a prophet of God. His original message seemed to be of one transcendent but personal God, the certainty of the Last Judgment, and social and economic justice. Muhammad said that God had sent other prophets (including Abraham and Jesus), but that the message given to him, called the Koran (meaning "to read"), was God's final, complete, and perfect revelation.

Other revelations followed. His wife and his cousin became his first disciples. The faith was given the name Islam, which means "submission to God," and followers were Muslims, "those who submit to God." Muhammad's revelations contained a strong message of social ethics, and his insistence upon improving the lot of slaves, orphans, women, and the poor earned him the enmity of Mecca's rich merchants. He and his followers were shunned and persecuted.

Then a breakthrough for the nascent religion: A delegation from the city of Medina, about 180 miles to the north, approached him and asked for his assistance in solving ongoing tribal feuds. In 622

C.E. (a date so important in Islamic history that it marks the start of the calendar, as the birth of Jesus does for Christians) Muhammad went to Medina, where he became not just a religious leader, but a ruler, judge, lawgiver, and military leader. Other Arab tribal leaders joined their allegiance to him, and he wasn't hesitant to use his authority to enforce Islamic principles among them. Mecca, meanwhile, continued to demand his extradition, and in this they were supported by Medina's Jews (foreshadowing the hostility against Judaism in the Arab world today). But Muhammad had amassed considerable power, and in a war he forced Mecca's surrender in 630. By his death in 632, he was the leader of a powerful Arab state.

Some of Muhammad's teachings were clearly borrowed from Christianity and Judaism. He taught the goodness, omnipotence, and unity of God. He urged generosity and justice in human relations. He warned of a final judgment, with paradise waiting for those who were found in God's favor. But other teachings, such as the pilgrimage to the holy city of Mecca, came from pre-Islamic paganism. Muslims assert that Muhammad himself was not divine (as Christians believe of Christ), but merely a human prophet. (This is why it is an insult to refer to a Muslim as a Muhammedan, which implies the worship of Muhammad rather than Allah.)

Four of Islam's five central duties—profession of faith, prayer, giving to the poor, and fasting—are familiar to Christians and Jews, since they're recommended not only in the Koran but in both the Hebrew and the Christian scriptures. Only the fifth, the requirement of pilgrimage to a holy shrine, has no cognate in Christianity and only a weak one in Judaism. In addition, Islam eschews alcohol and pork, and it encourages strong family bonds, sexual fidelity, and weekly attendance at worship. The goal of Islam (as in Judaism and Christianity) is God's ultimate rule on earth, and the goal of each devout Muslim is to do things that ultimately benefit humanity.

As you can see, there is more than a little common ground between the teachings of the Koran and the teachings of Christianity.

Yet if all of these good teachings—a concern for treating others well, a relationship to a loving, personal God—sound quite unlike what you have heard lately about Islam, then you have begun to realize the disconnect between what Islam was intended to be and what it has become in the minds of a few fanatics. Just as there are many kinds of Christians, each group of which may interpret the Bible slightly differently, so there are many kinds of Muslims. Just as throughout history some Christians misused our Scripture to justify war, slavery, and cruel monarchies, so some Muslims have used the Koran and its commentaries to advocate hatred, terrorism, and genocide.

Terrorism in the name of Allah does not represent the thinking of all the Islamic world—or even very much of it. Though I am no partisan of the Islamic faith, I believe we do an essential injustice to the Islamic religion when we represent all Muslims as terrorists—an injustice we would most heartily object to if someone were to describe all Christians in terms of, say, the white racist so-called-Christian survivalists that exist in some parts of the United States.

What happened to Islam after Muhammad's death is also parallel to what happened to Christianity in the centuries that followed Christ's ascension. Fights over power and doctrine factionalized Islam, and in the end there were a number of "schools" of Islamic thought, some that emphasized the Koran, others that emphasized the written traditions of Muhammad's life (the Sunna), and still others that placed much emphasis on logical reasoning or community consensus. The two best-known divisions of Islam today are Sunnite and Shiite. Like Christians who follow the Bible and yet have denominationalized over differences in tradition and biblical interpretation, so Sunnite Muslims stay close to the Koran and the Sunna, while having differences from area to area as to how to interpret and apply these authoritative teachings. Most Muslims are of the Sunnite branch of the faith.

Shiite Muslims (known to Americans through the 1979 kidnapping of Americans in Tehran by followers of Ayatollah Khomeini) have proven a somewhat more radical and unpredictable group, with less emphasis on the interpretation of the Koran than on original teachings supplied by powerful leaders—leaders who have proven adept at manipulating masses of Muslims.

Shiites are only one of many angry sects to have splintered off of Islam in the last century. The genesis of radical groups within Islam is not entirely the fault of the Islamic faith, but is at least partially attributable to the world in which most Muslims live.

In 1929 American theologian H. Richard Niebuhr wrote an important book called *The Social Sources of Denominationalism*. Written at the height of the ecumenical movement, which was also a time of strong emphasis on a social gospel as the solution for the world's ills, the book has often been criticized for reducing complex doctrinal schisms to simple matters of rich and poor, empowered and weak. And yet Niebuhr left us with an important understanding: Religion doesn't develop in a vacuum. People study and learn their faith in the context of a world in which they struggle for rights and privileges, in which power lies with one race or language group over another, in which basic freedoms are granted or denied, or in which there simply may not be enough food to eat. Christian theology has developed in the real world, and so has Islamic theology. And frequently, faith interpretations evolve to reflect people's needs, fears, and angers.

What we are only now beginning to learn is that despite the handful of princes and oil barons we see in the Islamic world, most Muslims are poor, have few opportunities, and little freedom. The nations that exist in the Arab world today are the creation not of the Arab people, but of colonialism and two world wars. (The boundaries of many of these nations were drawn quite arbitrarily in various conflicts during the nineteenth and twentieth centuries, mostly by Britain, Turkey, Russia, or France, all of which had interests in the region.) The monarchies, too, as we learned after the fall of the Shah of Iran, are frequently privileged despots favored by foreign governments for their ability to keep the taps of the Middle East's underground mineral wealth flowing.

While these facts are not an excuse for the anger brewing in the Islamic world against the West, they do help us to understand the reason it has happened. Take a huge mass of poor, disaffected, sometimes oppressed people with deep spiritual convictions; mix in just the right proportions of authoritarian religious leadership and Koranic theology that blames unseen enemies for all of your current problems and even advocates suicidal violence against them; and you have the recipe for social dynamite.

An example of such Koranic misinterpretation is found in the concept of *jihad*. The word is often mistranslated (in the West as well as in the Islamic world) as "holy war." The truth is not so clear cut: The word more properly means "struggle." The struggle, according to the Koranic commentators, is to reform the earth, with most of the emphasis on using political power to make the world a more godly place. This reform can encompass a wide range of good things, from explicitly religious activities and the teaching of morality, to enforcing good laws, to health and education. While there is a provision for the use of armed force in certain situations, never is one to carry out a jihad for political ambitions or for revenge, nor against innocent people. In fact, the part of the world with which Muslims are at peace is designated "The House of Peace" and is to be left alone.

Yet in the current climate of unrest in the Middle East, angry (though certainly very adroit) religious leaders have raised armies of jihad volunteers by promising revenge. Jihad has, by these teachers, been interpreted in its cruelest sense: permission to kill anyone whom you may wish to blame for your own bad situation.

Needless to say, such a flood of hatred does not stay between its banks. It overflows even into the society that generates it, which is why cruelty of despotic theocrats has struck not just those of us they consider infidels, but the Islamic people themselves. One of the things we have learned as we have focused on Afghanistan is that Koranic teachings have been so distorted that much of the cruelty of its so-called religious leaders has been expended on the country's own people. For example, Afghanistan's religious teachers during the past few years have replaced Muhammad's goal of kindness to women with a cruel misogyny directed against their own wives and daughters.

I have gone into so much detail on the subject of Islam to convince you that merely to say that the terrorists were Muslims, while it gives some specific content to their motivations, is not a sufficient explanation of the terrorists' actions. Despite the impressions we have received from a few news reports, most Muslim people were as appalled by these tragedies as Christian people were. The Koran does not permit, much less encourage, the kinds of things the terrorists did. So while the terrorists cited their faith as the reason for their actions, that explanation gives an inaccurate picture, and we must look one level deeper.

PEOPLE LIKE US

I must warn you that this is not going to be a very cheerful chapter. We are going to consider some of humanity's less-than-best qualities. But I must address this topic or risk failing to give you an essential warning about our human nature.

Although religion and politics contributed to what happened on September 11, 2001, it is my opinion that neither provides a full explanation. I propose to you that the problem is much more fundamental than that. The problem is a flaw in the hearts of people. As it turns out (and this is the less-than-cheerful part), this flaw can be found in the hearts of all people. Even you and me.

I remember once being approached by a church member after I had preached a sermon on sin. She stalked up to me, looked me in the eye, and said irritably, "All I ever hear from you preachers is how sinful we are. The truth is, I'm not that bad. I don't steal or kill or commit adultery. I don't hurt my children. I come to church and help the needy and contribute to charity. I'm not that bad! So why should I go around feeling like I'm a sinner all the time? Does God want us to constantly grovel like we're awful sinners, when we aren't?"

I wasn't entirely unsympathetic to her complaint. Because despite her outburst to me, she was indeed a good woman. She told the truth—she was a faithful wife, a participating church member, as well as a helpful, kind, and generous person.

Yet she may have misunderstood a couple of things about sin. First, that sin is a resident of every human heart in some degree, and second, that we have good reason to fear sin's potential. For the person who underestimates the power of sin is most in danger of it.

The apostle Paul warned us that "all have sinned, and come short of the glory of God" (Romans 3:23). What most troubles us about this passage is the inclusiveness of the word *all.* For it takes in everyone. Even people we don't think of as sinners. Ministers. Church leaders. Saintly grandpas and grandmas. Great humanitarians and philanthropists. The kindest, nicest people we know. Everyone has a germ of sin in them.

Most human beings have living in their eyebrows colonies of tiny insects known as mites. Babies aren't born with eyebrow mites but get them when we kiss and nuzzle them. When I first read about these mites, the thought bothered me a good deal. Who, after all, wants bugs in your eyebrows? I learned, though, that these minuscule critters do us absolutely no harm. They merely feed on waste skin and hair secretions. But neither can they ever be removed. They are a permanent part of our dermal ecology.

So it is with sin. Sin, introduced into our world not long after our creation, has become a permanent part of our spiritual ecology. Even those whom we don't see committing big sins still live in the world of sin. Even those who don't actively steal or kill must cope with a world in which there is much stealing and killing. So at the very least, sin presents every human being with questions to which there is no perfect answer. Do you punish children and thereby create unhappiness, or refuse to punish and risk a pattern of misbehavior? Do you eat food that isn't perfectly healthful when it is all you have, or refuse to eat and become weak? What is better: to refuse to kill for any reason or to go to war to protect the lives of innocent people? Do you tell a lie if it will save innocent lives?

Each of these questions speaks to how sin has invaded our world. For as long as there is no ideal answer to many of life's questions, then all human beings at one time or another find themselves making bargains with sin—even if they hate it.

So even a person who does not regularly choose to commit sins (if there is such a one) must be aware that there is more to sin than doing a bad action. Sin, says Paul, is also falling short of the glory of God (see Romans 3:23); and given the state of our environment and how strong sin is here, even the best people must admit that they have fallen short of God's glory. (In fact, I've found that the best of the best people admit it most readily, because their closeness to God has made them more acutely aware of God's perfection in comparison to human imperfection.) A very old Christian confession says, "Almighty God, we confess that we have sinned against You in thought, word and deed, by what we have done, *and by what we have left undone.*" Inasmuch as there is good to be done that we have left undone, we are sinners and in need of God's mercy.

Unlike eyebrow mites, though, sin is not benign. It does damage, and it does the most damage when we choose to participate in it. Most of us (and I suspect *all* of us) can remember situations when we knew perfectly well that what we were doing was wrong, but we did it anyway. We might have controlled our temper, but didn't. We should have turned away from that temptation, but didn't. Sin ceases to be a passive problem of threading our way through hard choices or of failing to live up to God's potential for us, and becomes something else altogether—an active participant in our spiritual lives. We're no longer making reluctant bargains with sin, but joining in a dance with it.

And here's the problem: It can happen to anyone. The more self-righteous you are, the more blind you probably are to your potential for evil. The devil, you see, isn't stupid. He is smart enough to understand our psychology and has been known to slip under the defenses of some of the best people around.

You have perhaps heard stories of the occult powers of Satan: of the devil appearing in person to people and destroying their lives. I have no doubt some of these stories have at least a grain of truth to them (though many, even those presented as factual in sermons and books, are surely titillating fiction masquerading as fact). When people speak to me about such appearances and express fear of it, I always warn them that Satan's temptations are going to be much harder to recognize than that. Satan knows that he wouldn't get anywhere with most people by appearing personally before them. That would send us running to the Lord! For ordinary folks like you and me, he gets much further by sugarcoating the temptation first.

When I was a boy growing up on a farm, we occasionally had to exterminate mice. One of the ways of killing them was with poison. Had we simply set out a bowl of arsenic, the mice wouldn't have been at all interested. To attract mice, you must put the poison on food that mice like to eat. If they like the nuts and grains you put out, they'll not notice that they are laced with poison.

So it is with sin. Satan always makes sin look good. If he didn't, we wouldn't be interested. He wraps a temptation to be morally impure in a warm relationship with an attractive person and suggests this justification: "Why shouldn't I have a little enjoyment in life? After all, my marriage isn't all that satisfying." He wraps a temptation to cheat on your taxes in the thought, "My family needs a little extra money, and if I don't keep it, it will just go to the government, and you know how they waste money." He wraps a temptation to get angry in self-justifying emotions—"I have the right to express myself, don't I?" It is only later that you may begin to realize how you've been deceived.

"Alright," you say, "I accept that all of us can sin. But you're making quite a jump between a person cheating on his taxes and a bunch of guys organizing to fly airplanes into the World Trade Center. I may be capable of the former, but there is no way I could ever do the latter."

This is perhaps the most frightening thing about sin: Its potential for insinuating itself into the lives of ordinary people and growing there is quite remarkable, and were it not for God's power holding it in check (those four angels of Revelation 7 that I told you about before), and God's power helping us to resist it, there is no knowing what we might be capable of.

In the 1920s a new leader came into power in Germany. In line with his usual methods, Satan wrapped his evil designs in what looked to most people like a young, promising, charismatic leader with energy, interesting ideas, and the skills of a master orator. Adolph Hitler seemed to say just the things that people most wanted to hear. He complained that Germany had been badly treated at the end of World War I (and perhaps he was right). The German economy was weak, and German society was suffering from a lack of order and discipline, he said. Most important, he told the people who their enemies were. When the Great Depression hit in 1929, he attracted millions of supporters by blaming it on a Jewish-Communist plot to destroy the German economy. There was no evidence for such a plot, but already-discontented people didn't need very much convincing. For years, Europeans' feelings toward the Jews had ranged from barely tolerant to openly hostile. While average Germans didn't persecute Jews (most happily did business with Jewish businessmen), they certainly had felt estranged from them. The unusual religious practices, languages, and appearance of European Judaism combined with jealousy toward wealthy Jewish bankers and financiers gave Hitler's accusations just enough credibility to convince many people and to silence many more. That is how thinly-defended hatred for one group of people became the operating principle for an entire society.

Notable is the role of German Christians in this conflict. Catholic and Protestant church leaders welcomed Hitler's leadership, saying that he would "bring clarity out of confusion, restore morality in place of decadence, and national self-respect instead of guilt and humiliation."[1] The church developed a theology to match the situation: To a people already primed to hate the Jews for economic and social reasons, it was relatively easy for skillful biblical exegetes to make a theological argument that the Jews' rejection of Jesus as the Messiah left them forever rejected by God, beyond the reach of salvation, and therefore not even really human. Some took the argument even further, accusing Jews of everything from cannibalism to devil worship to child-stealing. While some Germans were uncomfortable with the accusations, very few (including relatively few churchmen) actually rose to object when Jewish neighbors began disappearing. By this time, many were convinced that the *Führer* was on the right track. Wasn't the economy improving? Wasn't there a new swelling of national pride? And the result of objecting would have been severe anyway. "Who wants to die for the sake of a Jew?" argued many. "Whatever is happening may not be pleasant for them, but why should I put my family at risk?" It was a short step, then, to invite some of those same good Christian folks to take jobs as concentration camp guards and other tasks that contributed to the Holocaust.

The Reverend Martin Niemöller, a World War I U-boat captain who later became a Lutheran minister and ardent foe of Hitler, explained German apathy to the cruel treatment of minorities in German society in this way:

> First they came for the Communists,
> and I didn't speak up because I wasn't a Communist.
> Then they came for the Jews,
> and I didn't speak up because I wasn't a Jew.
> Then they came for the trade unionists,

and I didn't speak up because I wasn't a trade unionist.
Then they came for the Catholics,
and I didn't speak up because I was a Protestant.
Then they came for me—
and by that time no one was left to speak up.

There is a lesson for us in the experience of Christians in Nazi Germany. It is simply that ordinary people are, under the influence of extraordinary circumstances, able to do extraordinarily evil things. Most Germans were no different from most of us: They loved their children, they went to church, they worked hard, and they were responsible citizens. Yet in a time of extraordinary stress, and presented with beguiling justifications carefully presented to them in small doses, many found themselves doing things that they could never have imagined in more peaceful times.

Many of us have never fallen to extraordinary temptation simply because it has never been presented to us. And yet, in the crisis, I wonder whether we could trust our integrity. Said the prophet Jeremiah, "The heart is deceitful above all things, and desperately corrupt; who can understand it?" (Jeremiah 17:9, RSV). Without that perspective, any one of us would be capable of overestimating our own judgment, while underestimating the strength of the enemy, and thereby losing our hold on the Lord and our moral compass.

A connection to God is our only hope of resisting subtle temptation. Jeremiah compares that connection to a tree planted by a stream.

Blessed is the man who trusts in the LORD,
    whose trust is the LORD.
He is like a tree planted by water,
    that sends out its roots by the stream,
and does not fear when heat comes,
    for its leaves remain green,

and is not anxious in the year of drought,
for it does not cease to bear fruit (Jeremiah 17:7, 8, RSV).

It is this connection that serves to keep us from evil. Those who trust to themselves, or to human power and human understanding, are in trouble.

Thus says the LORD:
"Cursed is the man who trusts in man
and makes flesh his arm,
whose heart turns away from the LORD.
He is like a shrub in the desert,
and shall not see any good come" (verses 5, 6, RSV).

Without a connection to God, our goodness dries up, and we become surprisingly susceptible to temptation.

These examples point out that we actually have a partial understanding of the September 11 terrorists. Sin is our common weakness. The terrorists let sin take them further than you and I have. But if we consult our fears and hatreds rather than our connection to the Lord, then we, like them, are capable of greater evil than we have hitherto imagined.

I warned you this would be a dark and disturbing chapter, and I apologize if associating ordinary people with terrorists makes you uncomfortable. It would be much easier—and much more pleasant—to simply say, "Only *those* kinds of people are capable of such a thing." But my study of human history convinces me that all kinds of people—all races, all religions, all nations—are in extremity capable of taking counsel from our "desperately wicked" hearts.

By the way, this is not just a problem of countries or governments. In fact, it is always individuals who commit atrocities. When lots of individuals together commit mass crimes under a name (such as "the Nazi party" or "the Bosnian Serb government"), it then looks as if the responsible party is the group, not the people in it. But that is an illusion. Lots of people together committing a horrible atrocity under the leadership of some powerful leader doesn't absolve the individuals who participate from responsibility. History may name the Nazi party as the entity responsible for the Holocaust; in God's last judgment, though, it will be the people, from Hitler down to the lowest concentration-camp guard or the little old lady who could have saved her Jewish neighbors and didn't, who will be on trial.

After the war, German Christians and German pastors and priests were loud in making excuses for their part in the Nazi atrocities. Reverend Niemöller would have none of it, however. Understanding both the capacity for human evil and the interconnectedness of society that makes all human beings participants in it, he insisted that all of Germany must repent of Nazi crimes. In February 1946, ten months after Germany's surrender led to the full exposure of Germany's crimes to the world, Niemöller told a meeting of students in Erlangen, "I am responsible for what happens among the German people. . . . For we Christians in Germany have been guilty." Niemöller continued:

> Now six million Jews, an entire people, were murdered in our midst and in our name. When are we going to come to terms with this reality? If I were to ask one of you [concerning some particular atrocity], he would at once answer, "For that you must ask the local Nazi party headquarters.[2] What could *I* do?" And the local Nazi party headquarters will refer me to the regional party headquarters,[3] and so forth until we are referred all the way to national party headquarters.[4] And what will they say? Well, we hear it every day: they pass the buck to those three people who are happily out of the way: Hitler, Himmler, and Goebbels.[5]

Excuses will not do, said Niemöller. Though not every individual German was responsible for the Holocaust, all—even ordinary Germans who seemed to be minding their own business—were responsible for not stopping what happened at some point along the way. As the confession says, "We have sinned . . . by what we have done, *and by we have left undone.*" After the war, Niemöller helped to create the "Stuttgart Confession of Guilt," in which the German Protestant churches formally accepted guilt for their complicity in allowing the suffering that Hitler's reign caused.

Please don't misunderstand: I am not suggesting that it is somehow our fault that the September 11 terrorism happened. I am only suggesting that one of the best lessons we can gain from this event is to look within ourselves for marks of the same flaw—sin—that set these men on their road to destruction. It will serve us in two ways: as a point of understanding them (for honest people will find that they do understand one important thing about them, after all) and as a warning that we, like them, have unknown capacities for evil.

However, this kind of reflection probably can't be done on one's own, but only with the help of the Lord, who can "search the mind and try the heart, to give to every man according to his ways, according to the fruit of his doings" (Jeremiah 17:10, RSV).

---

1. John S. Conway, "National Socialism and the Christian Churches during the Weimar Republic, in *The Nazi Machtergreifung,* ed. Peter D. Stachura (London: George Allen & Unwin, 1983), p. 124.

2. *Ortsgruppenleiter.*

3. *Gauleiter.*

4. "Court Hall at #22."

5. Quoted in Frank Stern, "Evangelische Kirche zwischen Antisemitismus und Philosemitismus," in *Geschichte und Gesellschaft* 18, no. 1 (1992): 35.

The Impossible Necessity

You may still feel affronted by some of the similarities I've suggested between ordinary people (like you and me) and evil people. "I'll admit I'm a sinner," you may say. "But who are *you*, after all, to suggest that I should in any way be associated with people like *that?*"

I understand that feeling, and so I must hasten to clarify that just because sin is resident in us does not mean it must always flare up. A lesson from disease: Some microbes can exist in your body for years with no symptoms. Or they can manifest mild symptoms. Or they can take over your body and take your life. It all depends on the state of your immune system.

Jesus gave us a principle that, if followed, will provide immunity from the most severe flare-ups of sin. Whenever and wherever this principle has been set aside, it has led to the most horrible atrocities that human beings have ever perpetrated on one another. I can say without hesitation that it is the violation of this principle that allowed the September 11, 2001, terrorists to do such terrible things. And it is the violation of this principle that may cause ordinary individual human beings to do cruel and vindictive things to one another.

And yet this principle is very difficult to put into practice. It is this:

> You have heard that it was said, "Love your neighbor and hate your enemy." But I tell you: Love your enemies and pray for those who persecute you, that you may be sons of your Father in heaven (Matthew 5:43-45, NIV).

I remember my first enemy.

I grew up smack dab in the middle of the Cold War. I remember in the second grade looking at a picture in *The Weekly Reader* of an exploding atomic bomb. The accompanying article was about how many bombs America had and how many bombs Russia had. (Why some editor/educator felt compelled to tell this to small children, I'm not at all sure; but I think fear so permeated the culture of that era that it seemed to someone the right thing to do.)

Other things reinforced the fear of Russia. We had "duck and cover" drills in school. When the fire alarm went off, instead of going outside in an orderly manner (as in a fire drill), we went to the school cafeteria in the basement in an orderly manner, where we ducked our heads and covered them with our hands. In fact, every day, as we went downstairs for the "hot-lunch program" and had our little blue meal tickets punched, we could see on a basement door a goldenrod-colored sign with a design in the middle that looked like a flower with three very sharply triangular petals and the words "emergency shelter" on it. Of course, we all knew what that sign meant—this was the place we would hide when Russia dropped the bomb.

Nor were we safe at home. Our kitchen radio had similar triangle symbols at a 640 kHz or 1240 kHz on its tuning dial. The system was called CONELRAD (for CONtrol of ELectronic RADiation), an emergency broadcasting system for informing the American populace of the Russian invasion. Periodically someone would come on the radio station with tests of the emergency broadcast system, and each time I was terrified, certain that at last, Russia was dropping the atomic bomb. The announcer would say, "This is only a test," but I never completely believed him.

My grandparents, on the farm next to ours, lived in an old farmhouse with a damp-smelling, cricket-infested, dirt-floored room in one corner of the basement called the root cellar. Tucked away on a shelf was a box with that same yellow, three-petaled symbol on the outside. It contained a first-aid kit, some canned water, and canned biscuits. When they dropped the bomb, Grandma said, we'd hide in the root cellar and eat the contents of that box, along with the washtub of potatoes and shelves of canned fruit and dill pickles.

All of this preparation for disaster, it seemed quite obvious to me back then, was the fault of my enemy, Russia—a.k.a. the Union of Soviet Socialist Republics. I never imagined that any ordinary people like us lived in Russia—schoolchildren, parents, grandpas and grandmas, folks going about their everyday lives. I was pretty sure that it was an entire nation of bloodthirsty killers who wanted to destroy us; a whole country of snarling, growling soldiers, who spent all day despising Americans, for no other reason than that we were Americans. I imagined them living among huge, bulbous bombs that they could hardly wait to drop on us.

I wasn't sure why I was their enemy, but that's where things stood, and that's why I ran down to the root cellar when I heard a test of the emergency broadcast system on the radio and checked to see that the box of canned water and biscuits was still there.

If someone had told me back then, "You are to love your enemies," I would have felt two objections. One, that I didn't know them well enough to love them (and indeed, this is a constant problem with enemies—we hate them, in part, because we don't know them) and two, why should I love them if they don't love me?

My childhood enemy is gone. Collapsed of its own weight. All of those bloodthirsty warriors of the former Soviet Union look like plain, poor people now. As it turned out, most Russian people thought we were their enemy—and weren't sure why, either.

Now we have new enemies. And once again, Jesus asks us to love them.

That is extraordinarily hard to do. Imagine that you are someone whose loved one was in the World Trade Center when the first plane struck it. The one you love was never found. Someone says to you, "You have to love those very men who destroyed your father, mother, husband, wife, friend, sister, brother, or child!" I can understand if your initial reaction is, "I have no desire to feel love for such cruel people!" That is my reaction too.

So we must begin the process of following Jesus' advice with a good reason for doing so. And here is the best reason I can think of: If you hate the terrorists as much, and in the same way, as they hated you, you will become just like them. You will become emotional mirror images of them. Oh, you'll have your own justifications for feeling as you do, justifications that are quite unlike theirs. But make no mistake: The quality of hate is precisely the same.

Hate has two effects.

First, it destroys the hater. At first, people take a sort of perverse pleasure in their hate. It gives them a small comfort to think of revenge. But as time passes, the hate becomes a weight all its own. Like a ball and chain locked to your leg, you can't drop it, and you can't carry it. Martin Luther King, Jr. once wrote, "I've seen too much hate to want to hate, myself, and I've seen hate on the faces of too many white sheriffs, too many white citizens' councilors, and too many Klansmen of the south to want to hate, myself; and every time I see it, I say to myself, hate is too great a burden to bear."[1] Yet I have met people who spend their entire lives bearing that burden. Their small reward is their imagining that it hurts their enemy. Sometimes it does. But I have never seen a situation in which the hater is not damaged more badly than the one he or she hates.

There is nothing more corrosive to your own soul than cherished hate. That is true whether the hated one is Osama bin Laden or your brother-in-law. Whether Hitler or your next-door neighbor.

The second quality of hate is that it readily reproduces. Like a disease, it spreads through your entire life and into the lives of others.

I knew a man who for his entire life cherished hatred against his older brother. I don't know the details of the feud, though I believe it had begun as a conflict over the distribution of a minor inheritance. In any case, the event that precipitated it was fifty years in the past. The younger brother had been financially successful—he certainly had no more need of that small inheritance. Yet he persisted in hating his brother. His hatred consumed his life. He ruminated about it at home. He scolded about it when he visited with friends over coffee. He made a public show of his refusal to speak with his brother, to have anything at all to do with him—even though they attended the same church. As he grew older, the hatred filled all of his time. Even his children and grandchildren knew nothing of him but his obsession with his hatred for his brother. Though he wasn't quite sure what to apologize for—the small matter had been by this time so blown out of all proportion—the older brother made apologies to his sibling. Nothing would help, though; by this time the younger brother was absorbed in his hatred, and he couldn't let it go. Ultimately, he even dropped his membership in his church and spent his last years brooding alone at home.

If you hate someone at work, it will eat away at your spiritual health even at home. If you hate a relative, that hate will consume you years beyond the precipitating event. When families indulge in hate, the result is broken relationships and family feuds that last for generations.

And when nations or ethnic groups indulge in hate, the result is civil unrest or even war. Hate, like a virulent infection, spreads from heart to heart. People store up so many resentments against one another that even the simplest situations result in conflict. Nothing will satiate the haters but revenge. But the revenge only enlarges the circle of haters. Look at any trouble spot—Palestine, Rwanda, the drug war–torn regions of South America, much of the Middle East, the nations of the former Yugoslavia—and you will see how hatred has reproduced until it is a continual story of revenge met with revenge, met again with revenge. How can the cycle be broken?

Someone must stop the cycle. That means giving up the right to revenge, forgiving enemies, and stepping back from conflict. Sadly, in many parts of the world, ordinary, otherwise-good people have been so caught up in the cycle of hate that forgiveness seems an impossible price to pay.

Yet this is exactly why we who have been most hurt by terrorist attacks must be careful not to get pulled into the hate cycle.

Don't forget that in Jesus' definition, an enemy is not a person whom you hate, but a person who hates you. When He said, "Love your enemies," Jesus presupposed that you, as one who has given his or her life to God, understand the folly of revenge and have chosen to set aside your hatred. You cannot do that if you cherish even a smidgen of your hostility.

REAL PEOPLE

I was sitting in a cafe one day shortly after September 11, 2001, and overhead a conversation from the next table. "Those raghead idiots," said a voice almost hissing in anger. "We ought to bomb their sorry butts back into the Stone Age. Personally, I wouldn't care if they turned the whole region into one big radioactive bomb crater."

Here was a man who had identified the entire Arab world as his enemy. I have no doubt that if he had had his hand on a button that would send nuclear missiles to the Middle East, he would have pushed it. But, in fact, he knew nothing at all about his enemy. As he said those words, he wasn't picturing real people: women nursing babies, men laboring in fields, children going to school. The entire Middle East was to him a faceless group, and he blamed all of them for the recent disturbances in his once-contented world.

Jesus tried to address the problem of blaming faceless enemies by encouraging His followers to look at others as individuals rather than as a group. You may, suggested Jesus, think of them as neighbors.

The definition of *neighbor* figured prominently in one of Jesus' most memorable parables, the parable of the good Samaritan (Luke 10:30-35). To a Jewish person of Jesus' day, one's neighbor was a fellow Israelite. The Samaritans and the Jews had lived in the same land for many centuries, but they'd never gotten along. The difficulty stemmed from the fact that the Samaritans were almost, but not quite, Jewish. They shared common blood with the Jews, but they weren't pure in either ethnicity or religion. Their Scripture was a variant version of the Hebrew Scriptures. They worshipped at Mt. Gerezim, not at Jerusalem. Not quite foreigners and not quite family, Samaritans were more despised by the Jews than almost any other group.

But in Jesus' story, the Samaritan became a real person. He is not just a member of a group of anonymous people from Samaria. He is a man with a face. We can imagine him having a wife and children at home. He exhibits feelings and good intentions. He becomes, in short, a neighbor. Of course, what made the story so scandalous was that someone who was *not* a neighbor exhibited the behavior of one, while the real neighbors did not.

As we watch television, we see newsreels of masses of Arab people, walking about the streets and roads of their homes, shopping, going to mosques. They are dressed like one another, in clothing characteristic to their culture, but quite unfamiliar to us. Often they look similar to one another in hair and skin coloring. We know none of their names, nor very much about them. The backdrop in which we see them—the buildings, transportation, streetscapes, landscapes—are foreign to us. Their language means nothing to us. Do you see how easy it becomes to think of people as "those Muslims" or "those Arab people" and forget that they are, in fact, individuals with homes and children, hopes and faith?

Jesus, for His part, did not see Samaritans as a faceless group. When He met a Samaritan woman at Jacob's well, He treated her as a real person, not a member of an ethnic group. He took the time to become acquainted with her as someone with feelings, needs, longings, and aspirations.

If redefining enemies as neighbors seems difficult, consider what happened in New York after the September 11 attack on the World Trade Center. Many people observed that normally gruff New Yorkers became friendly and sociable, even on the subway. "We've got to stick together now," one man-on-the-street told a reporter. Having a common enemy made people into friends.

And we have a common enemy! Satan is our common enemy—he, and all the war, poverty, greed, selfishness, and hatred he has so successfully introduced into our world. If only we could stand together against Satan, we might not be so willing to war against one another.

LOVING THE UNLOVABLE

This is all so easy to talk about. But how do you actually do it? How do you love someone who is, well, unlovable? A woman said to me, "I know I'm supposed to love my ex-husband, but he hurt me so badly and did such horrible things to our family, that to feel any positive feelings toward him is almost impossible."

I think the answer to her question is found in understanding what Jesus means by "love."

• **Love is not romance, nor even necessarily friendship.**

Love is perhaps the most misused, abused, and misunderstood word in our vocabulary. I can say, "I *love* Häagen-Dazs dark-chocolate peanut-butter ice cream" (and I do), and then use the very same word when I say, "I *love* my wife" (and I do). The same word, but it means quite different things. My love for my wife is romantic and erotic and interactive, while my love for chocolate peanut-butter ice cream is nothing more than a strong preference.

While English has just one word for *love*, the ancient Greek language had several. When Jesus tells us to love our enemies, He refers to *agape* love—the kind of love God has. Agape love is an unusual kind of love. It doesn't have to spring from warm, affectionate feelings.

We know that God loves us—He's told us so. At the same time, He hates sin. He knows its destructive power. Sin is His enemy, and all who tempt others to sin, and all who persist in sin, are His enemies. His goal is to eradicate sin, and in the end He will do so, even if it means destroying sinners. So while God loves us, there are times when He doesn't like us very much. When we are horrible toward Him or one another, He doesn't prefer our company. In extended passages in the Old Testament, He makes His displeasure with recalcitrant human beings unmistakably clear.

Yet in spite of our frequent collaboration with His greatest enemy, God loved us enough to make the ultimate sacrifice. "God shows his love for us in that while we were yet sinners Christ died for us" (Romans 5:8, RSV). While we were in rebellion against Him—His enemies—He did the most incredibly loving thing for us that anyone has ever done: He gave His life for us.

Here He demonstrated a second principle about loving your enemies:

- **Love is not a feeling, but a decision.**

I read a story of a man who worked in an animal rescue shelter. It wasn't the kind of shelter that took in lovable kittens and puppies, but exotic wild animals that people had imprudently tried to keep as pets. These animals—ranging from pythons to tigers to raccoons—were often unsuited to be released into the wild. And yet they weren't tame, either, and they fought against being in captivity. "If I waited for the animals to show appreciation, I would never have been able to do the things for them that they required," he explained. The animals were ignorant of his feelings toward them, but he, wiser than they, took care of them because he knew that they were in need.

Dietrich Bonhoeffer was another German Lutheran pastor who lived through the Nazi era. Also an opponent of Hitler, Bonhoeffer, like Niemöller, was imprisoned. Unlike Niemöller, he did not escape execution. Some of Bonhoeffer's most profound writings addressed the great cost of being a disciple of Jesus Christ. In a commentary on "Love your enemies," Bonhoeffer writes, "By our enemies Jesus means those who are quite intractable and utterly unresponsive to our love, who forgive us nothing when we forgive them all, who requite our love with hatred and our service with derision. . . . Love asks nothing in return, but seeks those who need it. *And who needs our love more than those who are consumed with hatred and are utterly devoid of love?*"[2]

The words of Jesus remind us that this kind of love is quite out of the ordinary. "If you love those who love you, what reward will you get? Are not even the tax collectors doing that? And if you greet only your brothers, what are you doing more than others? Do not even pagans do that?" (Matthew 5:46, 47, NIV). The kind of love that one uses on enemies may not be the kind of love that rewards you with warm feelings. It may, instead, be the kind of love that permits you to say, "I did the right thing." I didn't get angry. I reached out. I helped. I was kind and generous and forgiving. And I did it even though I'm not feeling particularly affectionate toward my enemy right now.

• **Love grows from loving words and actions.**

We tend to think that what we choose to do is the result of how we feel. "I won't fix dinner, because I don't feel like it," we might say. Or, "I just feel like going out to dinner tonight." Yet one of the neglected principles of psychology is that feelings can follow actions. If you invest energy and prayers in someone, you may even begin to feel more positive feelings toward that person.

Jesus suggests that we learn to love people by saying kind words about them. Especially when they're not saying kind words about you! Should your enemy curse you, you will bless him in return. To his angry words, you give smiles. To his hateful thoughts, you try to think positive ones. To his insults, compliments.

By the way, your blessings don't need to be heard by your enemy to be effective. Even kind words about your enemy that aren't spoken to him nonetheless have two good effects. First, they change your own heart. They begin to sweeten your own inner bitterness. And as they change your heart, they'll change your attitude—and even the look on your face. Second, the kind words will pass through others, and eventually your enemy will hear them. You know how quickly gossip gets back to the one who is gossiped about. Why not replace that gossip with kind words? Let the grapevine buzz with good rather than evil!

Returning blessings for curses is possible because God has given you a spiritual defense against another's angry words or critical thoughts. He has given you self-confidence that is rooted not in any other person's assessment of you, but in the value He places upon you. While you were still a sinner, Christ died for you. That makes you incredibly precious to God—no matter what anyone else thinks of you!

Kind words are one way to bridge the chasm between you and your enemy. Jesus makes the task even harder by asking you to add good deeds to good words. "Do good to those who hate you" (Matthew 5:44, NKJV), He says. First we say positive words, and we must follow the words with loving actions.

But why must I be so good to someone who hates me? Bonhoeffer suggests that if we would really understand our enemy's need, we would know how much he needs our love. He writes, "There is no deeper distress to be found in the world, no pain more bitter than our enemy's. Nowhere is service more necessary . . . than when we serve our enemies."[3] Usually we are so busy with our own pain that we forget that the other person (and this is surely true of those in the Middle East who cherish hatred against us) is less happy than we are.

Yet there is no guarantee that when you love your enemy and bless him and do good for him, that he won't continue to spitefully use you. That's why Jesus gave us a fallback position. He said that if all else fails, no one can stop us from praying for our enemies. Even if we fail when we throw blessings back at him through his curses, even if we fail when we push our love through his wall of hate, even if our attempts to help him are met with ungrateful silence, we can still, through prayer, plead with God for him.

Bonhoeffer says, "For if we pray for them, we are taking their distress and poverty, their guilt and perdition upon ourselves, and pleading to God for them. We are doing vicariously for them what they cannot do for themselves. Every insult they utter only serves to bind us more closely to God and to them."[4]

- **Finally, loving your enemy doesn't necessarily mean being his doormat.**

A mother who had a drunken daughter said to me, "I keep rescuing her from every horrible situation she gets into. Night or day, if she calls me, I'm there. I just hope that one of these days she'll realize how much I love her and straighten out." Since the mother had used that strategy for forty years, with no sign of improvement, I tried to convince her that her actions toward her daughter were actually not very loving at all. The loving thing to do might well have been to give her daughter an ultimatum: either seek professional help or suffer the consequences of your choices. Unfortunately, neither mother nor daughter could find a new way of reacting to this life-long problem, and the daughter soon died of alcohol-related illnesses—but not before having drained her mother's health and happiness.

Remember that God loves us with an intelligent and just love. He has promised great mercy to those who reciprocate His love. But He will not, when all is concluded, honor insincerity and bad faith.

Few have wrestled with the difficulty of loving your enemy more eloquently than Martin Luther King, Jr. In the midst of the Civil Rights Movement, when numerous churches as well as King's own home had been bombed, when civil rights workers were being killed for their efforts to enroll Black voters, King continued to advocate peaceful, nonviolent protest. King wrote:

Somehow we must be able to stand up before our most bitter opponents and say: "We shall match your capacity to inflict suffering by our capacity to endure suffering. We will meet your physical force with soul force. Do to us what you will and we will still love you. We cannot in all good conscience obey your unjust laws and abide by the unjust system, because non-cooperation with evil is as much a moral obligation as is cooperation with good, and so throw us in jail and we will still love you. Bomb our homes and threaten our children, and, as difficult as it is, we will still love you. Send your hooded perpetrators of violence into our communities at the midnight hour and drag us out on some wayside road and leave us half-dead as you beat us, and we will still love you. Send your propaganda agents around the country, and make it appear that we are not fit, culturally and otherwise, for integration, but we'll still love you. But be assured that we'll wear you down by our capacity to suffer, and one day we will win our freedom. We will not only win freedom for ourselves, we will so appeal to your heart and conscience that we will win you in the process, and our victory will be a double victory."[5]

While he insisted upon love as the motivating power for change, he nonetheless insisted that things must change.

Loving your enemy takes sacrifice and effort. It is not easy, or it would not be agape love. Yet neither is it foolish and gullible. At times, even the use of force may be necessary. Yet even that, I think, can be done lovingly.

My big childhood enemy was Russia. Now we have a new big enemy. Unlike the old one, it is far more difficult to identify, for it has no single headquarters, nor single leader. We Christians are faced with the necessity of loving this new enemy better and more intelligently than we loved the previous one. That will not be easy to do.

And we are probably wise to begin by trying to love our local enemies. People who have hurt us. Those we tend to avoid. Those who have disappointed us.

You see, the little brother of hatred is disappointment. The little brother of hostility is everyday anger, unkindness, annoyance. It's the feeling when you hear the words, "We don't like your work. You're fired." It is the effect of overheard cruel gossip from someone you trusted. It is the emotional fruit of disappointing friends or loved ones who betrayed your faith in them. It is hearing, "Yes, I know I promised, but I changed my mind." It's being abandoned when you most needed support. It's the argument with someone you love that leaves you both seething and hurting.

If we will learn to love, we must start with our everyday enemies. Real disappointing people, whose faces we look into—colleagues at work, family members, friends and ex-friends, spouses and ex-spouses—these may be even harder to love than the enemies hiding in the dens of terrorism.

And as I write this for you, I find myself compelled by the words of Jesus, to line up my everyday enemies in my mind, see if I can't make them into neighbors—and then see if I could possibly think, speak, act, and pray love to them.

If you're trying to do the same right now, you'll realize that it is going to take extraordinary effort. Bonhoeffer again: "It cannot occur within the sphere of natural possibilities, but only when they are transcended."[6]

---

1. Martin Luther King, Jr., "A Christmas Sermon on Peace." In James M. Washington (ed.), *A Testament of Hope: The Essential Writings and Speeches of Martin Luther King, Jr.* (San Francisco: Harper Collins, 1986), p. 256.

2. Dietrich Bonhoeffer, *The Cost of Discipleship* (New York: Macmillan, 1963), p. 164, emphasis supplied.

3. Bonhoeffer, *The Cost of Discipleship*, p. 166.

4. Ibid.

5. Martin Luther King, Jr. *Strength to Love* (Philadelphia: Fortress Press, 1981), pp. 54, 55.

6. Bonhoeffer, *The Cost of Discipleship*, p. 169.

What About War?

One Saturday evening not long ago, I delivered a sermon at an alumni gathering of the Christian high school from which I graduated many years ago. In the audience were some of my fellow classmates from those years. I talked about the spiritual impact on all of us of the September 11, 2001, terrorism, including the revived interest in instituting mandatory military conscription in the United States—the draft. As I was speaking, I noticed that one of my classmates was crying. Afterward, another classmate explained our friend's tears: "She has teenage sons," she said. "I think you understand."

I did understand. All of us remembered the draft. As a teen I went to the Selective Service office in Jamestown, North Dakota, and there registered as a soon-to-be-of-age conscript. Those were the days of the Vietnam War. Thousands were going overseas, and some weren't coming back. I had no particular political convictions about the war itself. I only knew that my whole life was before me, and I didn't want it to end before I got a chance to live a little more of it.

While we loved our country, the family I grew up in didn't glorify military service. I had a great uncle who went down with the *USS Arizona* in Pearl Harbor and another uncle who served in Korea;

however, they weren't thought of afterward as ex-soldiers, but simply as family members whose lives had been interrupted (one permanently) by war. I was (and remain) a nonfighter, from a family of nonfighters, in a culture of nonfighters. Like many North Dakotans, my ethnic heritage is the German settlers who in the early 1800s fled Germany for the rich farmlands of the Russian Ukraine, primarily to escape military service. When, late in the nineteenth century, Russia tried to conscript them for the Russian army, they fled Russia for America. An old German man from my hometown used to joke, "When they drafted us in Germany, we went to Russia; when they drafted us in Russia, we went to the United States. And when they drafted us in the United States, we became Seventh-day Adventists." He was referring to the legal right to serve in noncombatant roles in the United States military that Seventh-day Adventists had earned early in their history.

It was as a noncombatant that I registered back in 1970, and for the next several years I carried a Selective Service ID card in my wallet. Each time I opened my wallet, I was reminded what might be in store for me. What made it worse was that we weren't quite sure why we were fighting. We knew that World War II had been to stop Germany's and Japan's effort at world domination. But the purpose of fighting in Vietnam was unclear to us. It meant only that some of our friends, after high-school graduation, would become soldiers, and a few would never return.

I remember the winter day in 1972 when I heard a classmate say, "Today's newspaper has the lottery in it." He wasn't talking, as someone would be today, about a state-operated game of chance to win a few dollars. The "prize" that day was getting drafted for Vietnam. During the latter part of the Vietnam War, conscripts were chosen by a birthday lottery. Each winter the year's 365 dates, representing the birthdays of young men turning eighteen, were drawn at random. Anyone whose birthday was in the top third of the list was almost certain to be conscripted.

I snatched the paper and scanned the list for June 20. I didn't have far to look. My birthday was number six, which meant I would be one of the first taken. All my plans suddenly faded. College would have to be put on hold. Or (if the worst happened) I might never have the chance of college at all. Nor getting married, having children, or a career.

A couple of months later, though, just before I would have been conscripted, President Nixon called the draft to a halt.

So when I saw my classmate crying, I knew she was remembering our school days, how the shadow of going to war hung over the heads of all her male classmates and wondering if the same shadow now hangs over the heads of her own sons. For since September 11, 2001, war has again become part of our lives. It is the story we listen for in each newscast. And an old question, quiescent in times of peace, has once more bubbled to life. How should Christians respond to war?

The Spectrum

We Christians are fond of saying that the Bible gives principles for every situation we face in life. Yet some of its directives are clearer than others. One topic on which you can find conflicting, and sometimes-contradictory, biblical positions has to do with attitudes toward war.

New Bible students are sometimes surprised to come across passages in the Old Testament that not only glorify but encourage war. "When you go forth to war against your enemies, and see horses and chariots and an army larger than your own, you shall not be afraid of them; for the LORD your God is with you," God tells the wandering Hebrews (Deuteronomy 20:1, RSV). God seems to be encouraging aggression against their enemies and promising His assistance against them.

What is even more surprising is how war seemed to be approached as a holy activity:

When you draw near to the battle, the priest shall come forward and speak to the people, and shall say to them, "Hear, O Israel, you draw near this day to battle against your enemies: let not your heart faint; do not fear, or tremble, or be in dread of them; for the LORD your God is he that goes with you, to fight for you against your enemies, to give you the victory" (verses 2-4, RSV).

The terms of defeat for the enemy were stern:

When you draw near to a city to fight against it, offer terms of peace to it. And if its answer to you is peace and it opens to you, then all the people who are found in it shall do forced labor for you and shall serve you. But if it makes no peace with you, but makes war against you, then you shall besiege it; and when the LORD your God gives it into your hand you shall put all its males to the sword, but the women and the little ones, the cattle, and everything else in the city, all its spoil, you shall take as booty for yourselves; and you shall enjoy the spoil of your enemies, which the LORD your God has given you (verses 10-14, RSV).

However, these terms were offered only in military adventures outside of Israel's territory—"the cities which are very far from you, which are not cities of the nations here" (verse 15, RSV). As for the people already occupying Palestine, God insisted upon total genocide. "In the cities of these peoples that the LORD your God gives you for an inheritance, you shall save alive nothing that breathes, but you shall utterly destroy them" (verses 16, 17, RSV).

There was no tolerance granted for the enemy's differing religious faith: they were to be destroyed so "that they may not teach you to do according to all their abominable practices which they have done in the service of their gods" (verse 18, RSV).

The passage betrays some disturbing values:

> When you besiege a city for a long time . . . you shall not destroy its trees by wielding an axe against them; for you may eat of them, but you shall not cut them down. Are the trees in the field men that they should be besieged by you? (verse 19, RSV).

Human beings, in this command, are of less value than trees. (Which sounds cynical to us unless we replace *trees* with *oil wells* and think of the Gulf War, at which point we may be able to understand!)

God even does some terrorism of His own. "Moreover the LORD your God will send hornets among them, until those who are left and hide themselves from you are destroyed" (Deuteronomy 7:20, RSV).

If this all sounds incredibly violent and merciless coming from the mouth of a God who has advertised Himself as loving and kind, who commands His people not to kill others (see Exodus 20:13), you can understand why Bible students have struggled with some of these passages.

Images of war also occur at the end of earth's history, when final victory for God comes through a series of battles, in at least a few of which the saints themselves, led by Jesus, have a part (see Revelation 2:16; 11:7; 13:7; 17:14; 19:11, 19). Revelation's picture of a great Middle-Eastern battle at "a place called in the Hebrew tongue Armageddon" (Revelation 16:16) has escaped its prophetic context: Armageddon has become eponymous in popular culture as the name for the anticipated political meltdown in the explosive culture of the modern Middle East.

Yet this picture of Jesus as a warrior-general seems quite unlike the Jesus of the Gospels—the One who steadfastly refused to take any political or military role. "I say to you, Do not resist one who is evil. But if any one strikes you on the right cheek, turn to him the other also," He says (Matthew 5:39, RSV). "Love your enemies, bless them that curse you, do good to them that hate you, and pray for them which despitefully use you, and persecute you" (Matthew 5:44, KJV).

Jesus consistently refused to advance His kingdom by force of arms. "My kingdom is not of this world," He said. If it were, "My servants would fight" (John 18:36, NKJV). He rebuked Peter for resisting arrest: "Put your sword back into its place; for all who take the sword will perish by the sword" (Matthew 26:52, RSV). (Since tradition says that Peter was martyred by crucifixion, the prophecy came true in quite a different way: Instead of the sword, Peter lived by the cross and died by it.)

Given this equivocal picture of war in Scripture, it should be no wonder that early Christians struggled to know what to do when asked (or commanded) to participate. A soldier who merely shouts blessings when the enemy is attacking would be of little value to an army. And yet Deuteronomy's portrayal of war seemed too incongruous with Jesus' teaching to be taken as a model for Christian military service.

Historically, Christian responses to war have fallen into three categories: pacifism, the crusade, and the just war.

Given the potency of Jesus' teachings for the early church, it shouldn't be surprising that pacifism was the church's first response to the problem of war. Most of the early church leaders, in the rare event that they commented on it at all, urged Christians not to take up arms. And there is no evidence of Christian soldiers until about 170 C.E.

Slowly, though, attitudes toward military service softened.

One of the reasons was that the highly efficient Roman military did a lot more than fight wars. Like the United States Army Corp of Engineers or the National Guard, there were units of the Roman military that served as police security or fire fighters, provided disaster relief, or even constructed large public projects such as bridges and aqueducts.

And as the church became a church of Gentiles, Roman soldiers began to take an interest in it. How can you refuse Christian fellowship to a soldier, especially if he's not engaged in active warfare?

As a result, pacifism as the absolute refusal to participate in any sort of conflict was softened. One of the earliest evidences we have of this is a third-century C.E. guide for church discipline called *The Canons of Hyppolytus*. *The Canons* said that military life was acceptable for a Christian, as long as he didn't personally kill people. Another early church leader, Origen, suggested that Christians do alternative service to soldiering, which could be anything that strengthens the moral fiber of society. It could even include praying for the success of the army that you refused to join!

The result was a sort of hybrid pacifism that has continued in the Christian church right up until today. Many of the Christian groups that encourage nonviolence—Seventh-day Adventists, Quakers, the Brethren churches, Mennonites—allow young conscripts to perform some kind of noncombat service for their government as long as they do not actively kill the enemy. These noncombatants have secured the legal right, when pressed into service against their will, to work as military medics or in other jobs in which carrying a gun is not required. Today pure pacifism—total noncooperation with the military aims of government—is rare, practiced only by a few Anabaptist groups such as the Amish.

So for the first centuries of Christianity, Jesus' example of nonviolence prevailed. Yet the story of Christians and war wasn't over. The second part of this story takes us to one of the main causes of the animosity of Muslims against Christians.

Shortly after September 11, 2001, President Bush referred to the military effort to stamp out terrorism in the Middle East as a "crusade." He and his advisors quickly had to apologize for their use of the word. Unlike in the Western world, where *crusade* can refer to any vigorous promotion (an "evangelistic crusade," for example), in the Muslim world it refers to a specific military action to force Christianity upon the Arab world. To modern Middle Eastern Muslims, the fear of a crusade is still very much alive and still arouses bitter feelings nine centuries after it first happened.

In the eleventh century C.E., an especially aggressive group of Muslims (the Seljuk Turks) began tightening their hold on their traditional territory and even pushing against the edges of Christian territory. Since the time of Jesus, European Christians had been able to make religious pilgrimages to the Holy Land. But when the Seljuk Turks captured Jerusalem and then went on to take over much of Asia Minor (modern-day Turkey, at that time the seat of Christianity in the east), Christian leaders became alarmed. In a sermon at Clermont, France, in November of 1095, Pope Urban II called for a holy war, or "crusade" (from the Latin for "cross"), to free the land of Jesus' birth from Muslim rule.

Europe's enthusiasm for the crusades surprised everyone. Over a period of two hundred years, there were seven major crusades called by the reigning popes and carried out by the nobility and their armies, as well as numerous smaller crusades that arose among the common people. Tens of thousands trekked to Asia Minor and Palestine to free the Holy Land from the rule of infidels.

The more successful crusades were self-financed by the nobility, and many crusaders even added to their wealth by trading along the way. Some crusades were not financed at all, leading to cruel consequences. A mystic named Peter the Hermit raised a crusade of 20,000 poor peasants, who left their homes and marched south with nothing more than inspiring ideals to fight with. Most were massacred by the Turks in Asia Minor, though Peter himself escaped. In 1212 a French boy named Stephen claimed to have received a message from Christ, calling him to raise an army of children to recapture the Holy Land. Children as young as six years old joined bands of children and traveled south. Some reached the Mediterranean and turned home when they found no one would give them passage to Palestine. Some went to Rome, where the pope, realizing this an ill-conceived notion, sent them home. Many died on the way. One group of children made it to Marseilles, France, where they did indeed get passage on a ship—to North Africa, where they were sold into slavery.

At least a few of the crusades succeeded. Initially, Christian soldiers won back both Asia Minor and Jerusalem and established some nominal Christian states there. Later, though, the Muslims regrouped under strong leadership, and by 1291 the last Christian stronghold in the Holy Land, the city of Acre, fell. And so ended the crusades.

Theologically, the crusades represented a theological shift from the peace-encouraging, freedom-respecting teachings of Jesus, to the Old Testament concept of holy war. The crusade knights and soldiers believed that mass killing to recapture Palestine was God's will. They marched into battle boldly, and sometimes suicidally, believing they were gaining not only glory for the Holy Roman Church, but a guaranteed place in heaven should they die. Not unlike the description of Israel's army in Deuteronomy 20, they did enormously cruel things in the name of Christ, from pillaging to killing entire cities of people.

The church even began to think of war, as Deuteronomy 20 seems to, as a holy act—an act of worship. Many knights joined a Catholic holy order of monk-soldiers called Templars, who were blessed by the church for the purpose of slaughtering those the church considered God's enemies—and did so with the name of Jesus on their lips.

If all this sounds familiar, that's because the motives sound not unlike those of modern Muslim terrorists! At least part of the problem that we're seeing now in our relationship to the Middle East is that Muslim terrorists see themselves engaged in a holy war and are willing to commit cruelty and commit suicide for a guaranteed place in heaven. It is hard to escape the conclusion that the theology of modern Muslim fanatics somehow reflects those of their Crusader enemies nine centuries ago.

FINDING MIDDLE GROUND

It seems to me that both ends of the spectrum—pure pacifism and the holy war—raise enormous questions for Christians.

Since September 11, I have occasionally heard Christian leaders imply that the United States is God's chosen country and that a war against Muslims is God's will. I always wince when I hear this, because I see no evidence that the Old Testament idea of a holy war still applies to Christians. Israel was a theocracy (a nation ruled by God), and as much as we may wonder about the brutal methods God used to overcome the former inhabitants of the land He promised His people, it remains that God was directly in charge of the political decisions of His people in a way that He is not for any nation today. No modern human president or general gets his orders directly from God, and if he claimed to, we would justifiably be very concerned!

While there are lessons to be learned from all parts of Scripture, there is much in the Old Testament that simply can't be applied directly to modern-day Christian believers. Vast sections of the Hebrew law codes, from building codes to criminal law, applied only to the theocracy of Israel. The relevance of these laws, except as examples of how God governed His people, disappeared along with the theocracy. God's holy people is now not a single nation or a single ethnic group, but a much looser confederation made up of all those who know Jesus to be the Son of God and allow Him to be Lord of their lives. God's church is not of one country or one language, but many. We are not even of one religious denomination. Not until God Himself brings us together at the end of time will we be united in one place for a pure and single purpose.

If God had meant for us to continue fighting holy wars, I have no doubt He would have renewed that call in the teachings of His Son, Jesus. Instead, Jesus taught His followers to turn the other cheek and to seek peace and avoid conflict. Even His statement that He did not " 'come to bring peace but a sword' " (Matthew 10:34, NKJV) wasn't about His followers defending Him, but the way in which His example of perfect goodness would inevitably divide good people from evil people.

As for pure pacifism, Jesus' teachings are abundantly clear. In most life situations, very little is accomplished by violence. Yet some Christians have suggested that there are values so important to us that when they are threatened, they must be fought for. Do you like freedom? I do too. Without it I couldn't worship as I do. I couldn't write books for others to read. Do you value peace and safety for yourself and your children? So do I. Do you wish for justice for those oppressed by pitiless tyrants? Me too.

So if you saw your central values threatened by someone who would, if possible, extinguish all you believe in, would you fight to defend them? If you encountered an enemy who was so completely without conscience that he would be willing to kill millions of innocent people without qualms, should you as a Christian take up arms against him?

Even some very thoughtful and dedicated followers of Jesus Christ have said "Yes" to that question. One of them was among the Christian faith's greatest theologians, Augustine of Hippo (354-430 c.e.). As he weighed what Jesus taught about nonviolence against the values Christians hold about preserving human life, peace, and freedom, he felt that there were situations in which armed resistance was necessary and justified. Theologians refer to this as the "just-war theory," and though Augustine was the first Christian to articulate it, he hasn't been the last.

Augustine said that a Christian could participate in wars that are fought to ensure justice and reestablish peace. He set the high standard that war against your enemy must be accompanied by love for your enemy. He further specified that Christians must carry on war in quite a different way from non-Christians: they must honor their promises to the enemy, respect civilians and noncombatants, and absolutely never engage in looting, burning, rape, or massacres. And unlike the Knights Templar of the Crusades, Augustine insisted that clergy and those in holy orders were not to take part in warfare.

Augustine apparently felt little satisfaction in articulating these teachings; scholars say his writings on the topic reflect a mood of gloom and resignation. He knew war to be irreducibly evil. When faced with war, the best we can do is to try to choose the slightly better of bad options, which will result in nothing more than the slightly better of bad outcomes. To Augustine, there was no glory or triumph in war, even though there were times when it was necessary to defend just causes.

The nation of which I am a citizen has already begun waging war in the Middle East. I pray we do not have to become any more deeply involved in war than we already have. I pray we will never again find ourselves so deeply immersed in war that we are compelled to conscript thousands of young people to fight and die. For even when it appears most necessary, war is a manifestation of evil—an evil I hope Jesus' return will soon make completely unnecessary.

Yet if the worst does happen—if we become embroiled in a war that calls for the sacrifice of more lives than we have thus far had to give, then what?

Neither I, nor any other Christian leader, is qualified to tell you precisely what choice you must make should you be called to participate in war. I hope I have made it clear that the idea of a glorious holy war to advance God's cause is theologically unsound, whether the warriors are Muslim or Christian. God is no longer leading people in war. Pure pacifism, too, raises many questions: Is it right to do nothing whatsoever to oppose the suffering of innocent people? That's probably why the two ideas that have come to define the center of Christian thinking on war are noncombatancy and the just-war theory.

Yet neither of these choices is thoroughly satisfying either. The thoughtful noncombatant will ask himself whether it is right for him to let others fight to preserve values he himself believes in. Is his choice to serve in a hospital rather than fight on the front lines based on his love for the enemy and his desire not to kill the enemy or on some less-noble motive? Many noncombatants have suffered much soul-searching as they saw friends returning from the front lines in body bags, wondering whether their choice not to fight was motivated by nonviolence—or merely by self-preservation. Further, is not working as a medic in a field hospital supporting those who do take lives? So is the noncombatant really promoting the ideals of Jesus just because he himself doesn't hold a machine gun in his hand?

Those who go to war believing that their cause is just are faced with even harder questions. Who determines whether a war is a just war? Many wars are deemed just and right by those who, from the polished halls of governance, order them fought. History not infrequently judges those same wars selfish or unnecessary, and the lives lost in them lost needlessly.

What of Christian principles? Can you be a good soldier without hating your enemy? Is it even conceivable that one could hold a gun to an enemy's head and pull the trigger while feeling love for him? Any reflective person who takes a weapon in his hands must be aware that the experience of killing another human being will leave a permanent scar on his soul.

The very act of war—even a just war—places otherwise-good people in moral quicksand. The American General William Tecumseh Sherman, perhaps the most pensive and ethically conflicted warrior ever to lead an army, wrote to a friend, "You cannot qualify war in harsher terms than I will. War is cruelty, and you cannot refine it." At a graduation address to the Michigan Military Academy in 1879 Sherman said, "War is at best barbarism. . . . Its glory is all moonshine. It is only those who have neither fired a shot nor heard the shrieks and groans of the wounded who cry aloud for blood, more vengeance, more desolation. War is hell."

Nowadays many warriors have the privilege of fighting wars while insulated from its consequences. A pilot who presses the button on a guided missile doesn't see the little child, too close to the target, whose skin is completely burned from his body and who dies in screaming pain while his mother holds him and weeps, happiness and hope draining from her soul. The man who drives the truck with weapons, the woman who works the communications equipment, the engineer who designs the missile, even the cook who far behind the lines prepares meals for soldiers—none of them have to see the splattered blood and pulverized limbs that their work makes possible.

Whichever choice we make, let us be painfully, startlingly aware of one thing: *War will result in someone's suffering.* So let us be sure that we do not spend a moment engaging in a sentimental glorification of war or of our fighting capabilities. Let us not hide behind our flag, spouting self-justifying clichés that seem to make the claim that God has confined His interests only to our side of the conflict. Let those of us who are Christians not use words like *revenge,* for even when fighting is necessary, revenge is precisely what Jesus intended us not to do. Let us never gloat over our victories or our enemies' losses. Let us not take joy in warmaking, because there is nothing at all joyful about it.

There are heroes in war and examples of great courage; but the entire enterprise is from beginning to end shadowed by the regret that it has to happen at all. The most that we can hope for from any war is a restoration of peace and justice with minimal suffering. But more times than not (and I believe this is becoming increasingly true as we come nearer to Christ's second coming), the results of even the most morally-defensible wars prove impermanent and unsatisfying. The only thing that can make it possible for a fully-aware Christian to fight in a war is the hope that the sum total of tears that will be shed because of fighting the war will be fewer than the sum total of tears that would have been shed had we not fought.

And those are sums that, short of heaven, we shall never possess the ability to calculate accurately.

A SIGN OF THE END?

This is the question that I've heard more than any other since the September 11 tragedy. I've had it asked of me many times. I've heard it discussed by believers in church and over lunch. I have heard it spoken of on Christian-radio talk shows and by preachers and teachers of many denominations.

Is this a sign of the end? Is this a sign that Jesus is coming again? Is it a sign that evil is increasing, and the end of all things that Christians have long anticipated is nearer than it once was?

The answer is quite simple: Yes, of course it is. How can it be anything else?

Let us, however, begin at the beginning. Why do tragedies like this lead us Christians to think about the second coming of Christ?

The basic answer is that Jesus said He would return to this earth and that when He did, He would bring earth's history to a close and establish His followers in a perfect kingdom—a kingdom in which God will "wipe away all tears from their eyes; and there shall be no more death, neither sorrow, nor crying, neither shall there be any more pain" (Revelation 21:4, KJV). Inasmuch as Jesus' first coming was the single most important event that has yet happened in the history of this world, inasmuch as He healed the sick, raised the dead, taught with intelligence and grace, laid the groundwork for our salvation, and demonstrated God's power over death itself, His promise to return again should be a highly anticipated event.

I remember sitting in a class in which the topic of Jesus Christ's return to this earth was being discussed. As the discussion proceeded, I saw an unsettled look on the face of one man. Finally he interrupted. "Listen, I'm not sure this is all that important. Why should I really care about Jesus' coming again?" He explained that he had heard of Jesus Christ's second coming since he was a child. It had been preached in his church, taught him in church schools, discussed in his Bible classes, and proclaimed at rallies and evangelistic meetings. For his entire life he had anticipated Christ's very, very soon return. He had studied current events, the "signs of the times" (Matthew 16:3), and had tried to make use of them to forecast final events. "I've watched things happen now for sixty years," he exclaimed, "and Jesus still hasn't come. So I've come to this conclusion: The main thing I have to worry about is my salvation. Jesus may or may not come, but I know that I don't have all that many years of life ahead of me, and when I die, the next thing I'll see is the face of Jesus. So I don't care anymore about Jesus' coming and the 'signs of the times'—only about having my own heart ready."

I understood what he was saying. And I wouldn't disagree with him that the state of his soul is important—whether he dies first or Jesus returns first. We Christians believe that salvation is a gift from God. We believe He gives us salvation, not because we are so godly, but for the sake of His Son Jesus' great love for us. We believe that only God has the power over life and death that is necessary to give mortal human beings immortal life. And yet the gift of salvation, and the power of salvation, will never be forced upon anyone. We can choose to accept it or to reject it. That is why we Christians invite people to give their lives to Christ Jesus one person at a time.

You can't accept Jesus for your spouse or your mother or your son. It is not a family decision, but a personal one.

We who know these promises surely want to go to heaven with Jesus. And we want our children and our friends and relatives to be saved too. But what I've come to see (and the latest terrorist actions have solidified my conviction) is that the need for salvation is so much larger than that. It is lovely for me to get Christ's grace applied to *my* life to ensure *my* salvation—but what about the rest of the world?

One December, at the party just before Christmas vacation, I watched a teacher hand out gifts to her class of first graders. These were nice children, but they weren't mature enough yet to understand that there was plenty for all. As the teacher brought out the gifts, there was greedy pushing and reaching and a chorus of "I want mine." "Me, too." "I want one too." And "I didn't get one yet!" "Kyle took mine! Make him give it back!" Those who managed to snatch gifts grasped them to themselves. Others were pushed back and became angry, and there were a few tears. Eventually the teacher had to send everyone—those who had already received their gifts and those who hadn't—to their desks, ideally to reflect on their own selfishness.

Sin is, in its essential nature, selfishness. By contrast, the grace that guarantees our salvation is God's free gift. And it is quite possible for recipients of God's grace to be selfish with the gift of grace! "As long as I and my people get our salvation, what should I care about the rest of the world?"

Then tragedies happen. Terrorists fly airliners into several major buildings. Criminals send anthrax-laced letters through the mail. Fanatics try to get their hands on nuclear weapons to vaporize their enemies. Our children march to war. And we, if we are thoughtful and reflective, will realize that it is not just us and ours that need salvation, but the whole hurting, broken, wounded, sick, mad world.

Somewhere, at this very moment, there's a young father dying in a car accident. Somewhere there are parents mourning a kidnapped, murdered toddler. There are parts of the world where thousands of mothers have in the last twenty-four hours wept over the starvation of thousands of babies. Somewhere a doctor is just now saying, "You have cancer, and there's nothing we can do." These are people like you and me, people whom these things hurt every bit as much as it would hurt you or me. We might not know these sufferers personally. They may be far from us. News stories—little more.

But when the evil strikes close to home, when we see the pain and suffering in our own back yards, then the reality of the awfulness of sin manages to pierce our contentment. Then we may try for just an instant to see the world through the eyes of others, to feel their sadness with them. Then we may begin to understand that our own problems and needs are symptomatic of an entire creation that is, as Paul says, groaning under the incredible weight of sin (see Romans 8:22).

If any good comes from the events of September 11, it is this: The tragedies may help you to set your sights on a salvation one size bigger than you alone need. A salvation that not only ends *your* suffering, but that simply ends *all* suffering. An extra-large salvation that fits everybody. An umbrella-policy salvation that covers everyone and everything in the entire world.

In the early 1800s, a New England preacher named William Miller became convinced that Jesus Christ was coming again. At the time, it was considered a novel idea; despite the frequency of the promises of Jesus' second coming in the Bible, Christians had forgotten it. Miller and his followers revived the idea—but with one major error: They thought they'd discovered the precise time when Jesus was coming.

Though they were wrong about the time, the idea of Jesus' soon coming didn't die. It remained the blessed hope of these Advent believers. Annie Smith wrote this hymn-biography of Joseph Bates, one of the most enthusiastic preachers of the Second Coming:

I saw one weary, sad, and torn,
With eager steps press on the way,
And long the hallowed cross had borne,
Still looking for the promised day;
While many a line of grief and care,
Upon his brow was furrowed there;
I asked what buoyed his spirits up,
"Oh this!" said he—"the blessed hope."

Joseph Bates didn't live to see Jesus return. Because he died a believer in Christ, he will come alive again at the resurrection to meet the Lord at His coming. His reward is secure. But Joseph Bates's blessed hope was not just that *he* would be saved. His hope was that the whole world would be saved; that this creation, and all of its wars and poverty and sadness, would finally be made perfect again. He wasn't content with a paltry me-size salvation; he and his fellow Advent believers had their hearts set on a universe-size salvation—the end of suffering and sin for every person on earth.

So are the events of September 11 a sign of the end? There is no doubt in my mind. This, and every other tragedy we read about in the news, are signs that our world needs saving and that Jesus still intends to come and rescue humankind. To take away all of our pain. To wipe the tears from all eyes. To end war forever. To give us a perfect home in a perfect place.

How Soon Is Soon?

There may, however, be another question hidden within the first one. When you ask, "Are the terrorist attacks of September 11, 2001, a sign of the end?" you may also be asking, "Does this mean the coming of Jesus is just around the corner? That it must happen within the next few days, weeks, or months?"

That is a more complicated question to answer.

The mistake made by those nineteenth-century believers in the advent of Jesus was that they thought they knew exactly when Jesus would return. Some sold all their property and invested it in evangelism. Some didn't make any provision for the future; they spent their savings and left their crops unharvested. On October 22, 1844, many thousands waited for the skies to open, for Jesus to descend on a cloud surrounded by the angelic hosts of heaven.

It didn't happen. And not surprisingly, the Advent believers were deeply disappointed.

Let's not be too critical of them. They understood the really important things about Jesus' second coming. They clearly understood the "why" of it; they wanted Jesus to come because they were intensely aware of the pain of this present creation and were longing for "new heavens and a new earth in which righteousness dwells" (2 Peter 3:13, NKJV). They understood the "how" and "where" of Jesus' return, for they taught that Jesus would return to earth "with the clouds, and every eye will see him" (Revelation 1:7, RSV). My reading of them and about them convinces me that they were well acquainted with the "who"—they were devoted to Jesus Christ as their Savior and longed to welcome Him as King. What they struggled with was the "when," and they were surely not the first in Christian history to do so.

Anticipation of God's sending a special messenger from heaven began soon after the entrance of sin. Bible scholars have long read the curse on the serpent in Genesis 3:15—"he shall bruise your head, and you shall bruise his heel" (RSV)—as a cryptic prophecy of heavenly assistance in defeating Satan. Several of the later prophets seemed to anticipate the Messiah, though none more clearly than Isaiah. His description of "a man of sorrows, and acquainted with grief" is among the most moving pictures in all of biblical literature. "Surely he has borne our griefs and carried our sorrows," writes Isaiah.

> He was wounded for our transgressions,
>   he was bruised for our iniquities;
> upon him was the chastisement that made us whole,
>   and with his stripes we are healed.
> All we like sheep have gone astray;
>   we have turned every one to his own way;
> and the LORD has laid on him
>   the iniquity of us all (Isaiah 53:6-8, RSV).

Isaiah's prophecy was correct right down to his vivid description of Jesus' trial and death.

> He was oppressed, and he was afflicted,
>   yet he opened not his mouth;
> like a lamb that is led to the slaughter. . . .
> And they made his grave with the wicked
>   and with a rich man in his death,
> although he had done no violence,
>   and there was no deceit in his mouth (Isaiah 53:7-9, RSV).

So although these Hebrew scholars knew a Messiah was coming, they still didn't know precisely *when* He would come. Prophecies in Daniel 9:24-27 might have given them clues to the time of His death had they understood the full implications of the Messiah's mission. But I prefer to be generous toward the Hebrew scholars and admit that we, too, have been able to interpret these time prophecies only because of the advantage of hindsight.

What the Hebrew Scriptures make unmistakably clear are the qualities of character that would identify the Messiah to His people. He would be humble and kind, helpful and generous. He would possess the power of God. He would teach the truths of God and call people to repentance. He would take our sins upon Himself.

Many people—especially the very religious people—missed all the cues. Far from appreciating Jesus' honest teaching and miraculous power, they constantly opposed Him. He ended His ministry "despised and rejected by men; a man of sorrows, and acquainted with grief; and as one from whom men hide their faces he was despised, and we esteemed him not" (Isaiah 53:3, RSV).

Yet not all rejected Him. A fortunate few (and not infrequently those who loved Him best were themselves the despised and rejected of humanity) knew Him, loved Him, and believed His claim to be the Son of God. It was to these that He gave the message that He would leave them and then later return (see John 14:1-3).

This message perplexed His followers. *He's here, after all, so why can't He just stay here and continue to teach and use His miracle-working power? Why should Jesus have to go away and then return?*

Had they read the prophecies, they might have understood that He was being obedient to the plan God had for Him. "It was the will of the Lord to bruise him," wrote Isaiah. "He has put him to grief." His leaving us as a human "offering for sin" would ensure that He could "bear [our] iniquities" (Isaiah 53:10, 11, RSV), and that would serve as His qualification to return "in clouds with great power and glory" (Mark 13:26, RSV).

And eventually He did leave them, with a final reminder that "this Jesus, who was taken up from you into heaven, will come in the same way as you saw him go into heaven" (Acts 1:11, RSV).

The "When" Question

It must be a comfort to those of us who wish we had a precise prophetic roadmap to the future to remember that even the disciples—the people who heard Jesus' teachings of the time of the end with their own ears—didn't know when He would return.

If the disciples had any timing in mind for Christ's coming, they surely thought Jesus meant to return while they still lived. That's because some of Jesus' teachings about the *eschaton*—the end of all things—seemed to indicate that His return would follow soon after His departure. Describing His second coming and the judgment, He says, "The Son of man is to come with his angels in the glory of his Father, and then he will repay every man for what he has done." Then He adds, "Truly, I say to you, there are some standing here who will not taste death before they see the Son of man coming in his kingdom" (Matthew 16:27, 28, RSV). In Matthew 24, after an extended description of signs and events we associate with Jesus' second coming, He assures them, "This generation will not pass away till all these things take place" (verse 34, RSV).

Some scholars think that perhaps Jesus was referring to His transfiguration in the first passage (see Matthew 17:1-8) and the destruction of Jerusalem in the second (see Matthew 24:1, 2). (In fact, for the disciples, the destruction of the Jerusalem temple might have meant the same thing to them as the time of the end— they could hardly imagine the world continuing if God had no temple in Jerusalem. But the temple was destroyed only a few years after this, in 70 C.E., while at least some of the disciples were still alive.)

Yet a misunderstanding of Jesus' words could have led to false hopes and disappointment. For the return of Jesus did not happen in their lifetimes—nor has it in ours. That's why we must remember that Jesus also warned that His return might be delayed. Before His coming there would be wars and rumors of wars, great tragedies, and Messianic pretenders, "But the end is not yet" (Mark 13:7, RSV). His end-time parables warn of delay: When the bridegroom didn't appear at the time anticipated, some of the wedding party went to sleep and half of them let their lamps go out (see Matthew 25:5). When a nobleman went on a long trip, he didn't return to check on his affairs when his servants expected him, but "after a long time" (Matthew 25:19, RSV). Before Jesus could return, He told them, at least one very, very large task had to be finished: The gospel must be preached to all nations (see Mark 13:10).

In fact, none of these passages are very helpful to us in pinning down precisely when Jesus will come. That's why we must take seriously His most important warning about the "when" of His coming. "Of that day or that hour *no one knows,* not even the angels in heaven, nor the Son, but only the Father" (Mark 13:32, RSV, emphasis supplied). If Jesus doesn't know when He will be asked to return, why should we suppose that *we* can figure it out? Jesus doesn't say, "Be ready by figuring out the hour of my coming." He says, "Be ready, because you know not the hour." Jesus is telling us that attempts to forecast the time of His coming are not the best use of our spiritual energy. The challenge is not figuring out the time; the challenge is becoming, and remaining, ready!

A man once said to me, "Jesus only said we couldn't know the day or the hour of His coming. However, I've figured out some prophetic numbers, and I've got the time of His coming pinned down to the month and year!" I confess disappointment in the misguided people who try to play those kinds of games with God's Word. His message is straightforward: It is not your spiritual task to try to forecast the time when Jesus is coming. Your spiritual task is to be spiritually ready, in heart and life, should He come today, tomorrow, or fifty years from now.

"But what about the signs of the times?" you might ask. "Didn't Jesus give some specific signs to look for?" Indeed, He did. In Matthew 24 He warns of false prophets and messiahs, of wars, of nation rising against nation, of famines and earthquakes, of persecution of believers, of some believers falling away from the truth, and of an increase in wickedness.

There is something particularly interesting about these signs: Virtually all of them have been happening in every age, in every society, since Jesus was here on earth! Those who were looking for them in 500 C.E. would have seen them somewhere on the earth. In 1000 C.E., a millennium after Jesus was here, people could have looked around them and seen wars, false religious claims, famines, and earthquakes. In 1500 C.E., the same would have been true.

And it is still true today. At every point in the history of the Christian church, some believer somewhere was suffering persecution—and they still are today. Other believers were becoming discouraged and falling away from the truth—and they still do. And through the entire 2,000 years of Christian history, there can be no question that wickedness has steadily increased. The "signs of the times" could be seen by Christians from 34 C.E. to 2002 C.E. At any point along the way, a thoughtful believer could look at the events around him or her and say, "Jesus told us this would happen. It means He's returning to end sin and take us home."

Jesus gave a message of hope that applied to all Christians, of all times. "Look for your Savior," the signs say. "He's returning for you."

But *when*, exactly? He didn't say. Rather than telling us precisely *when* to wait, He tells us *how* to wait:

> Watch therefore, for you do not know on what day your Lord is coming. . . . If the householder had known in what part of the night the thief was coming, he would have watched and would not have let his house be broken into. Therefore you also must be ready; for the Son of man is coming at an hour you do not expect (Matthew 24:42-44, RSV).

One morning my wife said to me, "Loren, we have company coming to our house tonight. Since you're getting home before I am today, would you please do these chores?" She listed several household tasks that needed to be finished. "Of course," I agreed. And I had every intention of starting them the moment I got home that afternoon. First, though, I collected the mail, in which I found my favorite magazine, through which I decided to page quickly before I turned my attention to tidying up the kitchen. Several articles caught my eye. Truly fascinating articles. "I'll just read this one," I thought.

"I'll have plenty of time before Carmen gets home, and even more time before the company gets here." But soon I was lost in another article, and I forgot entirely about the chores. From time to time, as the mantle clock chimed fifteen-minute intervals, the urgency of my work would press into my mind. But the lead sentence of the next captivating article would beckon me. My tasks would slip from my mind, and I went on reading.

Then I heard the garage door open. My wife was home. Earlier than I'd expected.

I flung the magazine aside and ran to the kitchen. I placed myself at the kitchen counter, took some dishes in my hands, and tried to look as though I'd been working hard there for hours—even mopping my brow with a tissue occasionally for effect.

She wasn't fooled. She couldn't have been. For one simple reason: The work wasn't finished. In fact, the chores quite clearly hadn't even been started!

I think Jesus hopes that the disasters of September 11, 2001, for all the pain they caused, will still have at least one good effect: They'll wake up His distracted people and get them busy at their spiritual chores. He wants happy, healthy, holy people, anxious to see Him again. What He never wanted was a bunch of lazy Christians sitting around waiting for the heavenly garage door to open before they decide to clean up their lives and be ready for His return.

Yet one thing is clear: There has never been, in all of earth's history, a time like this one. There has never before been a time when so many people are packed onto this globe. Never before have diseases been able to spread from one side of the world to the other in a single day. There has never before been a time when humanity has armaments capable of destroying all of us—and some of them quite possibly in the hands of suicidal fanatics. There has never been another time in all of history when we could communicate with one another so quickly and efficiently, while understanding one another so poorly.

Never before have so many people identified themselves and their group as wronged—and look for revenge. Never before have we had on this earth such a contrast between millions with more wealth than they know what to do with, and billions more without enough food to eat. At times it feels as if we're sitting on a huge lump of dynamite, just waiting for an explosion.

We are sure that Jesus' return is nearer than it ever was. But will it happen soon? I believe it will. I hope it will. And yet even the falling of great buildings doesn't help us to know exactly when. That's why His advice to live in the tension between everyday life (going to work, washing clothes, raising children) and the godly life (watching and waiting, hoping and praying, always keeping in mind that it could all change in a moment) applies just as much as it did a thousand years ago or two thousand years ago. "Let your loins be girded and your lamps burning," He advised, "like men who are waiting for their master to come home from the marriage feast, so that they may open to him at once when he comes and knocks. Blessed are those servants whom the master finds awake when he comes" (Luke 12:35-37, RSV).

As for knowing precisely *when* He will come, you can rest in this assurance: When it does happen, you'll know about it.

CHAPTER 9

THE ESSENTIAL INJUSTICE

On September 12, 2001, the Association of Trial Lawyers of America made an announcement that surprised everyone. "For the first time in our history," said ATLA President Leo V. Boyle, "the Association of Trial Lawyers of America, in this time of national crisis, urges a moratorium on civil lawsuits that might arise out of these awful events." The reason, said Boyle, was that "there are more urgent needs that must be served at this time"—healing, compassion, national unity, as well as "finding those responsible" and "taking the necessary steps to prevent its recurrence."[1]

There was a collective sigh of relief; America is a litigious culture, and no one was looking forward to years of argument about how many different people or companies could be forced to take some of the blame for the largest terrorist act in all of history.

The reprieve was short-lived. Within a month, the moratorium morphed into a legal-aid program for September 11 victims called Trial Lawyers Care, Inc., which, some critics darkly hinted, was simply a way of lining up business with potential plaintiffs. At the time I am writing, trial attorneys have hundreds of clients. They're preparing suits against anyone even remotely connected with these acts of terror: airlines, airplane manufacturers, security companies, managers and owners of the destroyed buildings, the United States government, and even drug-makers who might ever have worked with anthrax. Explained New York attorney Lee S. Kreindler, with a shrug, "This is our livelihood."[2]

While most of us groan when we hear tales of rapacious trial lawyers, that their vocation exists and even thrives says less about lawyers than it does human nature. We human beings want desperately to believe that there is a reason for everything; that someone, somewhere must be responsible; and that if we just search hard enough, we'll find someone on whom to blame our misfortunes. And, perhaps, make them pay.

Not surprisingly, God comes in for His share of the blame too. Insurance companies have labeled unforeseen tragedies, such as tornadoes, hurricanes, or falling trees "acts of God." The phrase suggests that God, because He is omniscient, omnipotent, and omnipresent, either made the tornado hit the house or might have stopped it, but didn't.

Sometimes, when folks tell me about the hard times they've faced in life, they'll add, "Pastor, I'm angry at God for not making my life better!" On one hand, I'm grateful for their honesty. I have no doubt that God understands our anger, and perhaps He even sympathizes with it. "As a father pities his children, so the LORD pities those who fear him," wrote David. "For he knows our frame; he remembers that we are dust" (Psalm 103:13, 14, RSV).

On the other hand, I want to come to God's defense. The implication is that God has been unjust. But because of what I know about the nature of evil, and of God's insistence on freedom for even His most recalcitrant children, I think it may be quite unfair to assign God the blame for our misfortunes.

WHOSE FAULT?

You've probably heard newscasts feature people who miraculously escaped the World Trade Center or the Pentagon, when circumstances indicated they should have been killed. Some escaped the building in the nick of time, falling concrete and fireballs at their heels. Some were surrounded by debris and dug out unharmed. Some were delayed in their commute to work in the World Trade Center that morning, or a minor illness kept them home. Others were supposed to be on one of the hijacked planes, but a schedule change shifted their flight time.

When I hear stories like that, I praise the Lord. Some were spared!

And yet I can hear someone else—a young husband whose wife was burned, the widow of a fireman crushed in the rescue effort, a child whose father was on American Airlines Flight 11—protesting, "Why did they get a miracle, and we didn't?" Why did one young father die, while another was miraculously spared? Why does one family have peace, while another is left with pieces?

I wish I had a totally satisfying answer for you. I told you earlier that we come up against our hardest obstacle when we ask God "why?" Why did one escape and another didn't? Why did God seemingly perform a miracle for this man and not that one?

I doubt there is a single big answer to these questions—at least an answer we can understand. Perhaps, though, what the Bible tells us about God can help us form a partial picture of God's perfect purposes.

• **God dispenses His blessings with surprising impartiality.**

The Bible makes it clear that God is wholly good and that He hates evil. My first assumption based on that would be to suppose God is going to do good things for good people, those who love Him and serve Him and honor Him, and let bad things happen to bad people.

And yet Jesus said that God is not nearly as discriminatory with His good gifts as we might suppose. Your Father in heaven "makes his sun rise on the evil and on the good, and sends rain on the just and on the unjust," said Jesus (Matthew 5:45, RSV).

Frankly, that hardly seems fair to me. I want God to be on our side! After all, we've been serving God. We're baptized members of the church. We pay tithes and offerings. We live good, honest lives. We are moral, upstanding citizens. We raise our children right. If there are Divine blessings to be had, shouldn't we have them?

But that's not God's way. He even blesses those who don't like Him.

An associate once came to General Robert E. Lee to ask his evaluation of a fellow officer. Lee replied that he thought him a good leader. "Really?" responded his questioner. "Apparently you don't know what uncomplimentary things he's been saying about you!"

"I do know," said Lee. "But you asked my opinion of him, not his opinion of me!"

God, because He is good and generous, finds reasons to bless even those who harbor poor opinions of Him. I don't know why. Perhaps He sees not what they are, but what they have the potential to be. Perhaps He blesses them simply because they are creatures made in His image and likeness. Perhaps He fears that blessing only those who love Him might lead to "cupboard love"—people who love insincerely, only for what they can get for themselves.

That's why I'm glad that God, not human beings, is the One who dispenses blessings. It took God less than a moment to see the implications of September 11 for every person in airplanes and in the paths of airplanes. And in that moment, He dispensed some blessings—in His own way, for His own reasons. Whether each person who received a miracle somehow deserved it isn't important.

- **Not everything that happens has a reason that you and I can discern.**

This may be a hard thing for some to accept. We want so desperately to believe that every event, every detail, is mapped out by God. That everything has a reason. That at the moment of the September 11 tragedy, He helped some and didn't help others, and that we ought to be able to figure out the reasons why.

It isn't that simple.

I remember standing with two farmers at the border of their two wheat fields. A severe hailstorm had passed through the night before. The wheat in the field to our left was hammered into the ground. Not a stalk, not a single head, was standing. It was a total loss. Yet the hailstorm had only skimmed the edge of the field on the right. A few stalks were knocked down, but most were standing. The farmer who owned the destroyed field was, understandably, dismayed. His neighbor, trying to lighten the mood, grinned and said, "I guess we can tell who's living right!" The ruined farmer managed a wry smile, but I thought he was wondering if perhaps his neighbor's joke had a little truth in it. "Is there something I did wrong," he may have been thinking, "that caused this to happen to me? Or something my neighbor did right that protected his field?"

In vain could he attempt to make a correlation. For he didn't get hailed on because he wasn't living right, nor was his neighbor spared because he was. The hailstorm was the result of high and low atmospheric pressure cells, temperature changes, and atmospheric moisture. Though God surely is capable of directing storms, the fact that meteorologists are able to predict storms' paths and severity tells us that generally God lets His creation operate according to natural laws. But because sin has corrupted creation, sometimes weather does bad things to good people, while less good people are spared. Such things simply happen, and if there is an immediate spiritual reason for them, it may well be one too complex for us to discern.

Shortly after the September 11 tragedy, some Christian leaders said that they knew God's reasons. The Reverend Jerry Falwell, pastor of the Thomas Road Baptist Church, said, "I really believe that the pagans, and the abortionists, and the feminists, and the gays and the lesbians who are actively trying to make that an alternative lifestyle, the ACLU, People For the American Way, all of them who have tried to secularize America. I point the finger in their face and say 'you helped this happen.' "[3] God has lifted the curtain, said Falwell, and allowed "the enemies of America to give us probably what we deserve."

But Mr. Falwell's theology is flawed. While it is true that this earth is deeply marred by sin, there is no way that anyone—even a noted Christian leader—can say with certainty that God is punishing the earth, much less that it is happening because he disagrees with human politics! Falwell's statement represents, as one CNN columnist noted, "a strange brand of Christianity, indeed"[4]—not unrelated, he suggested, to the kind "that would convince a suicide bomber to kill innocent people as a ticket to heaven." It is very dangerous to arrogantly suppose we know God's motives, "for God is in heaven, and you upon earth; therefore let your words be few" (Ecclesiastes 5:2, RSV).

Understand this clearly: The Bible leaves no doubt that there is a time when God will hand out blessings and punish evildoers. That time is not now. It is not while we live on this earth, but when our lives are over, when we stand before the judgment bar of God and are called into account. While there surely are consequences for sin on this earth, we do not live in a world in which moral actions and consequences correlate perfectly. Sometimes evil people are spared tragedy for no other reason than they didn't make it to the airport on time! Sometimes good people suffer and die simply because they were in the wrong place at the wrong time. Sometimes a hurricane destroys a city, affecting good and bad alike. Sometimes a disease sweeps through a country, killing its inhabitants without regard to their state of righteousness. Most of the tragedies that happen to us are not punishments, just as many blessings are not rewards.

We're not the first people to question God on these matters. Jeremiah complained to God, "I would speak with you about your justice: Why does the way of the wicked prosper? Why do all the faithless live at ease? . . . Yet you know *me*, O LORD; you see me and test my thoughts about you" (Jeremiah 12:1-3, NIV, emphasis supplied). At least in this instance, God seems to lose patience with Jeremiah. His response is short and cryptic: "If you have raced with men on foot and they have worn you out, how can you compete with horses? If you stumble in safe country, how will you manage in the thickets by the Jordan?" (verse 5, NIV). "Quit complaining, Jeremiah," He seems to say. "If you spend your time obsessing about questions like this, questions whose answers you don't really need to understand, you won't have the strength to face the real trials that are in store for you." Why some prosper while others don't is really none of your business!

The counsel God gave Jeremiah is good for us too. Trying to discern the answers to questions like this has the potential to fill us with frustration. God knows that often our limited minds couldn't understand the answers! Said Jesus, "Let the day's own trouble be sufficient for the day" (Matthew 6:34, RSV). There is enough for us to worry about without worrying about God's fairness.

- **God has a larger purpose on this earth than dispensing divine justice. His purpose is for all people, no matter their circumstances, to come to know Him.**

The Gospels tell of Jesus meeting a man who had been born blind. The Jewish teachers, ever looking to pick a fight with Jesus, asked His explanation for it. "Rabbi, who sinned, this man or his parents, that he was born blind?" (John 9:2, RSV).

The question presupposed that misfortunes on this earth are punishment for sin. They'd hypothesized that *someone* had to have displeased God, or God wouldn't have allowed such a debilitating condition to affect this man. Their question implied that a baby could sin within its mother's womb!

Jesus didn't accept their premise. "It was not that this man sinned, *or* his parents," He said. It happened that "the works of God might be made manifest in him" (verse 3, RSV, emphasis supplied). Then Jesus turned to him and healed his sight.

I have come to the hard conclusion that miracles are not always done for the person who most directly benefits from them. Sometimes they are done for no other reason than to showcase God's saving power.

I once met a man who'd had inoperable terminal cancer. His church had prayed for him, and God, by an incredible miracle, healed him. One would naturally assume that the miracle was done for him—to save him from suffering and death and to give him more time on this earth.

But a closer analysis showed something more had happened. As I studied the situation, it became clear to me that the healing had not benefited him as much as it had benefited others! Of course, he'd wanted to be healed. But he was a dedicated believer, and even had he died, his salvation was assured. He'd been financially successful, and his family would have been well cared for. What was most striking was how many *other* people who'd been struggling to believe had had their faith strengthened by his miracle. People who had doubted God's presence in their lives felt it again. Through this man's healing, God showcased His continuing power and presence in order to lead others to faith in Him.

Even tragedies can have a positive effect. I've met many people who returned to the Lord because the loss of a loved one or a terminal illness motivated them to seek answers to the hard questions of life and death. Death and misfortune, rather than miraculous healing, may bring people closer to God.

All of this is just to remind us that God sees our lives not within the brackets of our short years of life, but from the perspective of eternity. So to ask, "Why was this good man killed on American Airlines Flight 11, while his less-good (possibly even sinful) business partner overslept and missed the flight that day?" quite misses the point. It is not one individual's life, death, healing, or tragedy that concerns God, but the impact those events make on advancing His kingdom. And if my death, or yours, or a miracle that saves my life, or yours, should do that, He may well allow it.

- **As long as sin exists, we will look in vain for life's events to happen with perfect fairness. There is an essential injustice at the heart of our existence that will not be set right until God removes sin once and for all.**

One day my computer began acting very strangely. Occasionally (and I couldn't discern a pattern why it happened some times and not others) the letters I typed on my keyboard weren't the letters that appeared on the screen! It was terribly annoying and brought my work to a halt. Finally, after wasting many hours, I exhausted my own diagnostic ability and called in a friend who was a computer engineer. What he discovered was a computer virus. Someone, somewhere, had written a hidden program whose purpose was to vandalize any computer it came in contact with. It might have slipped into my computer with software or document I'd installed on it. But once there, it had begun to affect my computer badly, essentially making it unusable until my friend removed it.

Sin has thrown an element of uncertainty into our existence— a virus. While some things still seem to work as they were intended to (the laws of nature and mathematics seem still to apply), the moral and spiritual consistency of life seems to have gone awry. Bad things happen to good people, and good things to bad people. Good people can be hurt by the actions of bad people. Consequences don't seem always to fit motives. And what's more, that uncertainty will remain until God removes the sin virus that infects our entire earth.

Jesus told a story of a farmer who came out to his field one day to find his wheat strangled by emerging weeds (see Matthew 13:24-30). He recognized right away what had happened: An enemy had come at night and sown weed seeds in his field. For what purpose the enemy had done this, we're not told, but undoubtedly to cause unhappiness and loss to someone he hated.

The trouble, as the farmer explained to his workers, was that it wasn't as easy as simply pulling out the weeds, for they were rooted deep and would remove the wheat, as well. Instead, he counseled them to sort the weeds out at the time of harvest. Though their growing up together would surely stunt the growth of the wheat to some extent, waiting was the better of two bad options.

Sin is an interference in the functioning of the universe that will not be removed until the final judgment. Because of it, the normal operation of things has changed. We must take its uncertain effects into account as we try to understand the Divine calculus of good and bad, right and wrong, reward and punishment. Undoubtedly sin will do harm: Like the farmer's crop, the goodness of all creation has been stunted by it.

But we know that God is protective of His crop. There is a harvest coming! And then, at last, all will be made right.

- **Be assured that the essential injustices of this present world will not be allowed to stand forever.**

I have told you that these are questions to which we'll not have good answers until we can ask them of God. The good news is that we will get the chance to ask them of God.

My wife is a fan of English mystery stories, and occasionally she shares them with me. The plots are somewhat formulaic. A crime happens, often in a grand English manor house. The suspects are all in the room. Each has what might be considered a motive, and each has an alibi. A detective is generally on hand too (causing mystery-writer P. D. James to quip, "If the detectives in our stories really existed, who would ever invite them to dinner? Someone always gets killed just when they show up!") The detective is usually an enigmatic character him or herself, such as the innocent-looking spinster Miss Marple, the conceited continental Hercule Poirot, or the quirky esthete Lord Peter Whimsey. She, or he, is a master of observation and begins asking questions and gathering clues. By the time you near the end of the story, all the facts—clues, motives, and alibis—

are there. Yet it requires the detective, with his or her superior logical abilities, to demonstrate how all the parts fit together into a coherent story that points to the culprit. In spite of having all the same facts that the detective has, I'm usually not sure "whodunit" until I reach the last chapter, when the detective explains it all (usually in the drawing room of the mansion, with all the principle people gathered there). Then I say, "Ah ha! Of course! Now I see it!"

That's a bit like how I imagine the final judgment. God has already assembled all the data. Since God knows everything, there are no more clues for Him to discover. He sees the circumstances into which we were born and the events that have shaped us. He knows us intimately: the workings of our minds, our temptations, our dreams. He understands the role our own choices have played. He sees the big picture: how people, politics, wars, and culture have affected us. Sin, a wild card in our attempt to figure out the workings of the universe, is no mystery to Him.

So the final judgment is more than God's handing out rewards and punishments. The final judgment is when God brings all the facts and all the clues together. He will show how each event was part of all things working together for good to those who love God (see Romans 8:28).

The judgment will be reassurance that justice really has been done. The story will be complete. The mystery solved. And we'll live happily ever after.

- **Grace, too, is an injustice.**

I have often noticed that we human beings are much more likely to complain of injustices that affect us negatively than we are to give thanks for injustices that bring us blessings. For just as there are problems we didn't do anything to deserve, we also receive blessings that we really don't deserve.

One of those blessings is the gift of God's grace. "By grace you have been saved through faith," says Paul. And he takes care to add, "This is not your own doing, it is the gift of God—not because of works, lest any man should boast" (Ephesians 2:8, 9, RSV). The grace that casts our sins to the depths of the seas, overlooks our imperfections, and saves us for eternal life is something we never could earn. In fact, God gave the gift "while we were yet sinners" (Romans 5:8, RSV). There was no justice in God having to come to this earth in Jesus Christ: it was His gift to us. There was no justice in Jesus Christ having to die for our sins: it was His gift to us. And there is no justice in our receiving salvation, for it is totally undeserved.

So while we live in a world where we will suffer difficulties we don't deserve, let us never forget that God has also given us gifts we don't deserve. And the most important of those is His willingness to forgive us and take us home to heaven with Him.

I wish I knew something that would bring each hurting, questioning person, each one who lost a loved one in the 9/11 terror, perfect assurance of God's perfect justice. Of course, I can't do that. We have no choice but to wait to ask God our hardest questions face to face. In the meantime, we have the promise that God is watching us. He is following each detail of our lives. "Are not two sparrows sold for a penny? And not one of them will fall to the ground without your Father's will" (Matthew 10:29, RSV). As long as there is sin in the universe, He cannot rescue every sparrow—nor can He rescue the people He loves so much, who "are of more value than many sparrows" (verse 31, RSV).

But we know He is there. Watching. And, I am certain, with a very sympathetic heart.

---

1. From ATLA's Web site, www.atla.org.
2. *Business Week Magazine,* November 12, 2001.
3. Remarks on Pat Robertson's *700 Club* television program, September 14, 2001.
4. Bill Press, "American Ayatollahs," CNN.com, September 27, 2001.

Keeping Your Balance in an Unbalanced World

I don't know when I first noticed it. At first it was only a subtle vibration I could feel at high speeds in the steering wheel. I thought it might go away on its own. But a few hundred miles later, the vibration had turned into a full-scale *thump, thump, thump*, accompanied by some other even more disconcerting squeals and rattles. I knew something was wrong.

The guy in blue coveralls at the tire shop confirmed it. "That wheel is badly out of balance," he said, "and has begun to knock everything out of line. You need to have it repaired." And if I didn't? "It will eventually keep wearing the tire, the wheel bearings, and drive train until it ruins everything." A few repair dollars later, and I was back in business.

Our world has developed a decided *thump* lately. It has actually been giving us warnings for some time, but when other parts of life are going well, we don't pay much attention. We try to ignore the problems; perhaps they'll go away. But September 11 has brought the awareness of the world's brokenness back to our attention. Since that September morning, we have become intensely aware that this old world is badly out of moral balance.

And yet here we are. Trying to live on this globe, which is even as we speak *thump-thump-thumping* with exploding bombs and shells and squealing and rattling with the multifarious sounds of human strife.

Someday it will be repaired. But for the moment, we have to keep living here, trying to keep our balance in an unbalanced world.

Here are five strategies to keep your life together even when the world seems to be coming apart.

1. Conquer Worry

Of the person who tells you he *never* worries—that he proceeds through life sans care, apprehension, or any sort of disquiet of the spirit—you can be sure of one thing: He is not telling the whole truth. Everyone worries. And so I do not suggest (as some have) that one who trusts in the beneficence of God will never worry, even should buildings tumble and airplanes fall from the sky. Of course he or she may worry. Even Jesus, faced with His own execution, suffered fear and anxiety. Until we are taken to that promised place where we are threatened by nothing and no one, where all of our doubts are completely eradicated by the fulfillment of God's promises—until then, we will have moments of worry.

And yet I am convinced that there are realities, accepted on faith, that make a believer's worry of a different quality from those of non-believers. Faith in God can soften the blow of life's slings and arrows.

In the wake of September 11, I returned to a text that I have known from childhood and long ago committed to memory. But though I knew the text so well and assumed I understood it well, this time it yielded to me a new and unexpected understanding.

"Come to me, all who labor and are heavy laden," said Jesus, "and I will give you rest. Take my yoke upon you, and learn from me; for I am gentle and lowly in heart, and you will find rest for your souls. For my yoke is easy, and my burden is light" (Matthew 11:28-30, RSV).

We labor under heavy loads of worry and care. So many souls are filled with rest-less questions. Will there be a war? Are we ever again going to be safe in America? Will someone I know get hurt or killed? What is going to happen to the economy?

When I returned to this familiar text, I noticed something I'd not seen before. I saw that the burden Jesus offers us is the one He's been carrying. And it is a light burden!

This tells me one thing: Jesus is not as worried as we are! He is not worried about the future. He is not worried about war. He is not worried about the Middle East. He is not worried about the stock market. He is not worried about the time of the end. That is because Jesus knows that by the mercy and grace of His Father, in the end every problem will work out for good.

What is the burden Jesus is carrying, that He invites you to take from Him? His burden is simple: nothing more than "Trust God." Trust Me. Trust My Father. Trust Us with your cares and concerns and questions. Trust Us when We promise that all things will work together for good to those who love Us.

And that's the burden Jesus invites you to take! Lay down your worries, because they're not going to do you a smidgen of good, and take Jesus' burden instead. Spend your mental energy on one thing: exercising trust in Jesus and His Father.

Why is it that Jesus doesn't have as heavy a load to carry as we do? Why is He less worried than we are? Because Jesus has already endured the worst the world has to offer. He has suffered martyrdom and by the power of His Father proved that even death could not defeat One who belonged to God. That's why He's not worried. He endured the worst that Satan could dish out (worse than we will ever have to face) and found it not nearly as scary as it seems, especially when you're looking back at it from heaven.

Note that the text doesn't say that Jesus is going to pick up your burden—your worry, your care, your fear. He asks you just to drop it. It is worthless. Jesus has no use for your worries. He tells you to drop your burden and pick up His. For the burden that Jesus carries is lighter than the one you carry.

So let our Lord keep His eyes on the affairs of the world, because He has infinite power to direct them toward a good end. As for us, "Let us fix our eyes on Jesus, the author and perfecter of our faith" (Hebrews 12:2, NIV). We may have a war. Let us keep our eyes on Jesus. More terrorism may happen. Let us keep our eyes on Jesus. The stock market may go down farther and the economy plunge into recession. Let us keep our eyes on Jesus. Someone we know may be hurt or killed in these conflicts. Let us keep our eyes on Jesus.

There are so many things about this broken world we cannot repair ourselves. We are not in control. But one of the things our faith assures us is that God *is* in control, whether or not we understand His methods.

2. Practice the Art of Acceptance

Once you place your trust in God, He'll enable you to take another step away from worry. Those who trust in God begin to accept life here as it is, for what it is, with all of its limitations and problems. And with that acceptance there rolls off of us the huge burden of trying to remake the world into the place we wish it would be.

Back in 1942 a New York member of Alcoholics Anonymous brought to the attention of his support group a caption in a routine *New York Herald Tribune* obituary that read, "God grant me the serenity to accept the things I cannot change, the courage to change the things I can, and the wisdom to know the difference."[1] Everyone was immediately struck with the power and elegance of these few short phrases, and before long it became one of the official prayers of Alcoholics Anonymous.

The beauty of this prayer is the way it expresses the difficult balance between the necessity of changing those things that our effort and decisions can affect, while accepting those we cannot change. For surely there are aspects of life that we can and should choose to alter. God has given us the ability to choose to be kind and helpful, to control our selfish urges and suppress our worst tendencies, to make decisions that will help us to grow in character and goodness.

Yet there is so much that is out of our control. For example, other people, who also have freedom to make their own choices; world affairs too distant from us to affect; incurable illness; and a multitude of intractable problems. And those who spend their lives trying to change things over which they have no control sacrifice peace of mind. The strategy for peace of mind is not to fret over the unchangeable, but to know what we cannot change and instead make the most of those parts of life that we can change.

While most people know the first part of what Alcoholics Anonymous has labeled "The Serenity Prayer," many are unfamiliar with the last part.

> Living one day at a time,
> enjoying one moment at a time,
> accepting hardships as the pathway to peace.
>
> Taking, as He did, this sinful world
> as it is, not as I would have it.
>
> Trusting that He will make all things right
> if I surrender to His will,
> that I may be reasonably happy in this life
> and supremely happy with Him forever in the next. Amen.

The prayer acknowledges something that has at times been hard for people to accept: that the best we can hope for in this old world is to be reasonably happy. Supreme happiness is reserved only for the next world. As for right now, we must at times take this sinful world as it is and trust that Jesus, who knows our world intimately, will someday make all things right.

The quality of acceptance required for serenity embraces all parts of life, right up to and including death. In Shakespeare's play *Julius Caesar*, Caesar observes,

> Of all the wonders that I yet have heard.
> It seems to me most strange that men should fear;
> Seeing that death, a necessary end,
> Will come when it will come.[2]

The Bible is equally blunt. While the dead "know nothing," "the living know that they will die" (Ecclesiastes 9:5, RSV). And yet knowing that, how often do we practice accepting that reality and preparing for it?

Experts tell us that even in the wake of September 11, we are in less danger of being victims of terrorism than we are of many more ordinary perils—from car accidents to heart attacks. Yet the shock of seeing people like us murdered in so exaggerated a gesture has stimulated us to spiritual reflection in a way that car accidents have not. It is no wonder that we have thought deeper and longer thoughts in recent days than we did before that Tuesday morning in September.

Perhaps this is what the psalmist meant when he recommended that we "number our days" (Psalm 90:12)—that we consciously think about how much of life we have left and live accordingly. When we are young, we never think of death. Even as we grow older, we become adept at denying its approach, even as we know the remainder of life is shortening. And yet all of us (unless Jesus should come in our lifetimes) will die! This very day may be my last! Shouldn't, then, one of our most important tasks of reflection be to keep ourselves always conscious of the shortness of life and so live what's left with the right priorities?

So teach us, Lord, to number our days. For we must accept that life is short. Especially when compared to eternity.

3. Don't get too at home here

I have a friend whose husband has a particularly mobile job history; he has spent his adult life relocating from city to city for his vocation. Because he is happy in his work, extraordinarily kind to her, and an excellent provider to boot, his wife has adapted herself to his peripatetic ways. A stay-in-one-place nest-builder myself, their manner of life I find impossible to imagine. "How are you able to uproot yourself every year for a move to a whole new city?" I asked her. "Simple," she says. "You make yourself as comfortable and at home as you can—but you never unpack all the boxes."

That's the kind of attitude a believer needs to take toward this world. As comfortable as it seems at times, this world is not where we're stopping. An old gospel song expresses the attitude this way:

> This world is not my home; I'm just a-passing through.
> My treasures are laid up somewhere beyond the blue.
> The angels beckon me from heaven's open door,
> And I can't feel at home in this world anymore.

Jesus prayed that His disciples, though they were "in the world" would not be "of the world"; they would be, in a manner of speaking, resident aliens (see John 17:6-19). It is extraordinarily difficult to live in the world, but not be of the world. So much of us is invested here! Our friends are here. Our possessions are here. Our houses are here. Our wealth is here. We know that the world is flawed, of course. We become painfully aware of the world's temporariness when great tragedies happen. Then, at least for a while, we long for something better.

But having lived nowhere else but the world, it is extraordinarily difficult for us to be here but not really feel that we belong here. We want to stay. We want to unpack all the boxes. This is, after all, the only life we've ever known.

In Hebrews 11, the author offers a gallery of Scripture's greatest people of faith. When I first really studied the people listed, I was surprised. Those I found there didn't match my picture of a faith-filled life. Most experienced great difficulties. Abel, in spite of his faithful sacrifice, was murdered. Noah faithfully built the ark that saved all living things, yet his family story ends with an almost unimaginable moral problem. Abraham had moments of spiritual greatness, but he, too, lied and cheated to get his way with Pharaoh; and his nephew Lot's family demonstrates a totally dysfunctional family with a concluding X-rated chapter. Isaac was tricked, and tried to trick others in return. You remember Jacob and his deceit of Esau. Moses was, among other things, a murderer.

Don't forget Rahab. Not only was she an immoral woman, but she earned her commendation of faith for becoming a traitor to her own people and watching all of them die in the rubble, crushed as a whole city of buildings fell on them.

Samson, the Bible's bad boy, is on the list. A fellow who did very little right in his life except at the end, when he became a suicide killer. Faithful David was a man of considerable vanity and a murderer to boot. Samuel was more than just an obedient lad who grew into gentle high priest; if you read 1 Samuel 15, you'll find him a man whose hands were stained with blood.

Also on this list of faithful people is Jephthah. He is the illegitimate son of a prostitute, kicked out of his home by his father who rejects him. As an adult he somehow gains enough reputation as a military leader that he is asked to lead an army against the Ammonites. Jephthah has the total fanaticism of a terrorist. He vows that if he is victorious, he will sacrifice to God the first thing he sees when he returns home. Unfortunately, the first thing to greet him when he gets home is his daughter, and so he kills her. He murders his own child.

These are the people that Hebrews calls faith heroes! Why? Surely not because they led charmed lives! The things that happened to them are the kinds of things we hope will never happen again! We hope for a world where no cities fall, where no child is killed, where there is no more war, murder, or suicide. We hope for a place where there is no uncertainty, no crying nor tears nor any pain, where the former sufferings are no more because God has made all things new. We hope for life beyond this life. A city whose architect and builder is God.

And at this point we see that not one of those things is true about this earth! All we have is a promise! The reality has not happened.

And so it was with these heroes of faith. Hebrews says, "All these people were still living by faith when they died. They did not receive the things promised; they only saw them and welcomed them from a distance" (Hebrews 11:13, NIV).

There are moments of happiness on this earth. But as long as evil things are happening anywhere, even if your home is a place of perfect peace, your happiness is flawed too. And then sooner or later evil touches you. It will. It always does. No one goes through life without being touched by pain. That's why verse 13 says faithful people feel themselves to be "aliens and strangers on earth" (NIV).

And so this is the prescription for a life of faith: Believe with all your heart that a better world *will* come. Then begin living there in spirit, even while your physical body is anchored down here.

How do you do this? Jesus gave clear instructions: You invest in heaven.

A while back a stockbroker recommended I invest in shares of a biotechnology company. I really didn't know a lot about biotechnology, but I took his word that this company had a solid record and would grow. So I instructed him to make the purchase. Once I was a stockholder, I became interested in the stock. I followed it every day in the newspaper. Now I never visited the firm's laboratory or factory. I didn't even know exactly where they were located. Yet because I had invested in it, I was interested in the company. A bit of my heart had followed my money, and I hoped the company profited.

It is this very phenomenon to which Jesus was referring when He said, "Where your treasure is, there will your heart be also" (Matthew 6:21, KJV). Investments on this earth always have a limited life span. "Do not lay up for yourselves treasures on earth, where moth and rust consume and where thieves break in and steal," said Jesus (Matthew 6:19, RSV). All our possessions are temporary. Even if they aren't destroyed, death will separate you from them. The car you have so lovingly protected and polished and kept rust-free will be driven away by a stranger. The home you have decorated and kept spotless will be someone else's home. Yet even the new owners won't get to keep these things forever. Someday "the day of the Lord will come" and then "the elements will be dissolved with fire, and the earth and the works that are upon it will be burned up" (2 Peter 3:10, RSV). Nothing from this earth—not even the most precious gem or the most valuable work of art—will last into eternity.

That is why Jesus made another investment alternative available to you. "Lay up for yourselves treasures in heaven," counseled Jesus (Matthew 6:20, RSV). When you start investing that which is of most value to you—whether time, money, or energy—you will begin to follow the value of your "shares"! Your interest will be in the progress of God's kingdom!

How do you invest in heaven? You do it by giving what you value most to the work of God.

Television commercials, billboards, and magazine advertisements suggest that one's investment should be in oneself: a nicer car, a bigger house, better clothing. This old world (in which, we have agreed, we are but temporary residents) would try to make you think that there is no higher use for your money than to spend it on yourself. I have become convinced that the best way to counter that attitude is simply to give money to good causes. To your church or good charities. The act of giving, with no thought of personal gain, reinforces the understanding that this world is not our home, for no investments made in it will last eternally like investments made in God's work: the relief of suffering and the salvation of souls.

Grandma was approaching her seventieth birthday, and her family wanted to do something special for her. Her small house was already full of knick-knacks and gadgets. She had no need of clothing or appliances. She didn't much care for flowers. So they needed to come up with a unique gift. Then someone remembered that there was one thing Grandma had never done: Grandma had never ridden in an airplane.

When the idea was first suggested, Grandma was appalled. You see, Grandma was a rather large woman, and she was certain that no machine could ever lift her bulk into the sky. Her children reasoned with her, however, and arrangements were made for her to take a ride in a Cessna at the local airport.

When the birthday arrived. Grandma took one look at the little red-and-white, four-place Cessna setting on the tarmac, and said, "It will never get me off the ground." As the pilot looked on and chuckled, her children pleaded and cajoled. All Grandma would say was, "It will never get me off the ground." In the end, though, her children's arguments prevailed, and with some wiggling and squeezing and pushing—because Grandma really was quite a substantial woman—she was finally made comfortable in the airplane.

When she arrived safely back on the ground, the family clustered around to get her reaction. "What did we tell you, Mom?" her son said. "It did get you off the ground!"

"Don't think you're so smart, young man," replied Grandma. "It wouldn't have, except that I never put my full weight down!"

Those who live in expectation of heaven never quite put their full weight down on this earth. For this world is not their home. And so the joys here never totally delight them, nor the tragedies take them entirely by surprise. They have known all along that there is something better to look forward to, for they have already claimed their citizenship in a city "whose builder and maker is God" (Hebrews 11:10, RSV).

4. Think of Satan as a defeated foe

Oh, he's still firing darts of temptation at us. He's still trying to destroy those God loves. But his are the acts of a desperate being. "The devil has come down to you in great wrath, because he knows that his time is short!" (Revelation 12:12, RSV).

God has assured us that in the end He will win the war. But in the meantime, Satan occasionally wins a battle. Sometimes the battles he wins are discouragingly devastating and painful. That's what happened to the World Trade Center and the Pentagon. That's what happened when Ugandan president Idi Amin killed his own people, when Hutu and Tutsi people slaughtered one another in Rwanda, when the Khmer Rouge rebel army killed millions of Cambodians, and when the Nazi regime gassed millions of Jewish people.

And on a more personal scale, that is what happens when a young mother dies of cancer, when a marriage breaks up, when a car crash kills a child, when a thief breaks into a house. Each and every one of these says just one thing: that Satan is still fighting against God, and sometimes (more often than we like) he wins a battle.

The book of Revelation, in a revealing metaphor, describes a time when a Rider on a white horse appears on this earth. It is clear from the first that this heavenly General means business: "With justice he judges and makes war. His eyes are like blazing fire, and on his head are many crowns. . . . He is dressed in a robe dipped in blood" (Revelation 19:11-13, NIV). Heavenly armies—billions and billions of angels—follow Him (see Revelation 19:14). Out of His mouth comes a sharp sword "with which to strike down the nations" (verse 15, NIV).

At first, His enemies aren't sure who He is. "He has a name written on him that no one knows but he himself" (verse 12, NIV). And then the name emblazoned on His robe becomes clear to them: "KING OF KINGS AND LORD OF LORDS" (verse 16). This heavenly General is none other than Jesus Christ, appearing at His second coming!

And His patience with Satan's terrorism is at an end.

Satan does not surrender. He gathers together all his followers— every wicked king and president, every terrorist, every criminal, all those who loved selfishness and hated God—to make war against Jesus Christ and His followers.

But the battle is short. Satan is captured and imprisoned "to keep him from deceiving the nations anymore" (Revelation 20:3, NIV). Later, the destruction of evil will be complete, when Satan is thrown into the lake of burning sulfur, and fire comes down from heaven and devours all who followed him (see Revelation 20:9, 10).

And that is the end of terrorism. It is the end of war, of hatred, of ethnic violence, of genocide and homicide and suicide. It is the end of all of the hurtful, sad things, large and small, that Satan has caused to happen.

As for God's people, they've learned their lesson forever. Sin will not arise again, for God has made everything new—including us. "He will wipe every tear from their eyes. There will be no more death or mourning or crying or pain, for the old order of things has passed away" (Revelation 21:4, NIV).

5. LIVE IN HOPE OF THE RESURRECTION

A man woke up one morning and realized that his life had become decidedly dull. He puzzled about it for a while and finally decided that what he needed was a vacation. He had always been a homebody, not a man who enjoyed the unexpected, and the thought of an exotic trip was a bit intimidating to him. On his way to work he passed a travel agent's office. He stepped in and explained his situation. The travel agent listened intently, a smile on her face. "So you see," he concluded, "I want to do something that will shake me out of my rut. Not just an ordinary vacation, but someplace unusual."

The travel agent pulled out a brochure for a vacation to Nepal. The potential traveler found himself enchanted by her descriptions of the unusual culture of the people, the rugged geography, the unfamiliar foods and fragrances and sights he would see. But then he began thinking of how his stomach might actually react to that unusual food and his lungs and ears to the high altitude, not to mention a plane ride of many, many hours. And the trip suddenly seemed too much for him.

"I'd like to go," he said. "But it frightens me, too. I guess I'm not as adventurous as I thought I was!" He considered for a moment. "But perhaps I'm being hasty," he said. "Before I back out of this completely, give me your best reason for thinking someone like me can take a trip like this."

"I just got back from there myself," said the travel agent. "And if I can do it, so can you!"

No one I know has ever been to the other side of death. Yet we Christians have a description from a good authority—from the mouth of One of us who has been there—of what we will find there. It is a country that we have not visited, but not one with whose spiritual geography we are wholly unacquainted. One of us—a very good, very reliable One of us—has made the journey. And He has assured us that all will be well. And He has promised to see to it that we get there safely, and that when all accounts of life on this earth are settled—when we look back from the shores of heaven—we'll be satisfied that "our present sufferings are not worth comparing with the glory that will be revealed in us" (Romans 8:18, NIV).

In the meantime, we have to keep on living on this old earth. If the journey to the other side is frightening, so is living here. In case we should forget that undeniable fact when life is going well, Jesus reminded us, "In this world you will have trouble" (John 16:33, NIV). And of course, He was right. Sometimes, when we are happy and content, we forget that we are under spiritual siege. The terrorism in American cities is only the latest (though hardly the last) reminder that in this world we may experience a great deal of trouble.

There are no assurances that only good things will happen to us on this earth. Some of us may even die from Satan's terrorist attacks. "What if I had been in one of those airplanes?" asked one of my friends after news of the crashes. She shuddered. "It could have been me."

"Yes," I admitted, "it could have been any of us. But if it had," I was able to assure her, "you would have seen a fiery crash, and the next instant you would be alive again, looking into the face of Jesus—with all fear and sadness gone forever!"

The things that may happen in this world are truly terrible to contemplate. But when God gets done shaking this earth, He will shake out all the bad stuff. All the bad stuff in the world and all the bad stuff in us. We will find ourselves in a place that cannot be shaken, filled with people that cannot be shaken. Not by sin or war or earthquakes or airplanes crashing into buildings. Nothing will shake that place out of balance. It is the one place of perfect stability, perfect peace, perfect goodness. There will be no CNN in heaven. No NBC nightly news. And no need for them. For there will be no breaking news of tragedies.

Now, it seems to me, is the time for believers to practice all that stuff we've talked about all these years. About trusting God in the hard times. About believing that all things work together for good to those who love God. About how these present sufferings are no match for the glory that is to come. About how not even a sparrow falls without the Lord's knowledge. About how He clothes the lilies of the fields, and will He not much more care for you, you of little faith?

On the other side of death is the New Jerusalem, the city of the living God, and thousands upon thousands of angels. On the other side of death is infinite peace and security. On the other side of death, there is no poverty, no pain, no sickness, no suffering. On the other side of death, I'll see those I love again.

Best of all, on the other side of death, my Savior waits. The first to prove that by the power of God, we can have victory even over death. I will meet Him beneath a grand tree on the lawn of heaven, along with millions and millions of others—even some who died on September 11, 2001. He will lift His hands above us in welcome and gratitude and blessing. And we will read there the assurance of His love for us, written indelibly on the palms of His hands.

---

1. No one knows for certain the origin of this prayer. American theologian and pastor Reinhold Niebuhr took credit for it, though he also admitted he may have borrowed the idea from earlier sources. See www.aahistory.com.

2. *Julius Caesar,* Act II, Scene 2.

If you enjoyed this book, you'll enjoy these as well:

Time of Terror, Time of Healing
David B. Smith. How do we make sense of the senseless? The names of Columbine, Oklahoma City, and New York City conjure up images of intense suffering and despair. Does God care? And what is He going to do about it? David B. Smith explores our darkest fears and delivers some much-needed hope in this timely book
0-8163-1912-X. Paperback.

Let Not Your Heart Be Troubled
Randy Maxwell. Using the words of Jesus and Bible writers as a guide, Randy Maxwell leads us on an inspirational journey to assurance in troubled times. Find refuge from worries about terror, death, God's love for you, the end, and more in this little book that encourages us to cling to Jesus in the storms of life.
0-8163-1915-4. Hardcover.

Searching for a God to Love
Chris Blake. Packed with lively stories, intelligent dialogue and believable hope, *Searching for a God to Love* is a one-of-a-kind sharing book for family members, friends, and acquaintances who have drifted from God, or simply have never found a God they could love. Now they will.
0-8163-1719-4. Paperback.

Order from your ABC by calling **1-800-765-6955**, or get online and shop our virtual store at **www.adventistbookcenter.com.**
* Read a chapter from your favorite book
* Order online
* Sign up for email notices on new products